W9-BWL-652

WHAT IS THE CHURCH?

IS VOLUME

48

OF THE

Twentieth Century Encyclopedia of Catholicism

UNDER SECTION

V

THE LIFE OF FAITH

IT IS ALSO THE

77TH

VOLUME IN ORDER OF PUBLICATION

Edited by HENRI DANIEL-ROPS of the Académie Française

WHAT IS THE CHURCH?

By ANDRÉ DE BOVIS, S.J.

Translated from the French by R. F. Trevett

HAWTHORN BOOKS · PUBLISHERS · *New York*

© 1961 by Hawthorn Books, Inc., 70 Fifth Avenue, New York 11. Copyright under International and Pan-American Copyright Conventions. Philippines Copyright 1961 by Hawthorn Books, Inc. All rights reserved including the right to reproduce this book, or portions thereof, in any form, except for the inclusion of brief quotations in a review. This book was manufactured in the United States of America and published in Canada by McClelland and Stewart, Ltd., 25 Hollinger Road, Toronto 16. It was originally published in France under the title *L'Eglise et son mystère, Librairie* Arthème Fayard, 1961. The Library of Congress has catalogued the Twentieth Century Encyclopedia of Catholicism under card number 58-14327. Library of Congress Catalogue Card Number for this volume: 61-17756. The Catholic University of America Library has catalogued this volume based on the Lynn-Peterson Alternative Classification for Catholic Books: BQT184.T9v.48/BQT2188. Suggested decimal classification: 230.2.

First Edition, November, 1961
Second Printing, October, 1962

NIHIL OBSTAT

Joannes M. T. Barton, S.T.D., L.S.S.

Censor Deputatus

IMPRIMATUR

E. Morrogh Bernard

Vicarius Generalis

Westmonasterii, die VIII SEPTEMBRIS MCMLXI

The Nihil obstat and Imprimatur are a declaration that a book or pamphlet is considered to be free from doctrinal or moral error. It is not implied that those who have granted the Nihil obstat and Imprimatur agree with the contents, opinions or statements expressed.

CONTENTS

INTRODUCTION

A book must not be required to do what it is not intended to do. The present volume is not intended as an "ecclesiology". Other authors have devoted themselves successfully to this undertaking. Dr Schmaus, for example, has written eight hundred pages on the subject in his *Katholische Dogmatik*, while Mgr Journet has judged it possible to allot no less than two thousand to it in his *L'Église du Verbe Incarné* (translated into English as *The Church of the Word Incarnate*). It would obviously have been foolhardy to attempt to emulate these large works in a mere one hundred and fifty pages.

I have therefore limited their scope. In any case, the latter was defined by the title I had been given: "The Church and her Mystery." The book's subject is essentially the "mystery" existing in the Church.

It is this mystery alone which I have attempted to throw into relief. Explanations and analyses refer to it alone. Hence there is no treatment here of historical or apologetic problems. Thus the primacy of Peter is not considered in itself, and the holiness of the Church is dealt with far more from the theological than from the historical standpoint. It therefore follows that there is no broad statement of the thought of dissident Christians. There are only brief, formal allusions which do not allow full justice to be done to doctrines and intentions.

Even the question of the mystery of the Church has been shorn of many of its aspects. I say nothing, for instance, of tradition, of the homogeneous development of dogma, of the doctrine that there is no salvation outside the

Church, of the problem of the Church's members, and all these are questions which would have involved a reference to the Church's mystery. Rather than mention every point cursorily, I have preferred to concentrate attention on one alone, the mystery of the Church as she is in herself. God willing, this should help us to be more conscious of this mystery and to understand it better.

The Church has been in existence for twenty centuries. She shows a determination to go on existing. Not that there have not been all sorts of troubles of a kind to discourage her from surviving. Even within her own bounds there have arisen storms which ought to have annihilated her. But she still exists.

It would therefore seem that over a period of twenty centuries mankind should have been able to form a not too fanciful idea of what the *Catholica* is, just as it has succeeded in acquiring a reasonable notion of the shape of Africa and of the movement of the stars. But far from it. Without risk of exaggeration it might even be said that, of all human communities, the Church is the one that gives rise to the most characteristic, the most persistent and the most divergent misunderstandings.

THE OUTWARD APPEARANCE OF THE CHURCH

The Church as a visible phenomenon is an amazing thing. It may well be that we are too accustomed to it to take due notice of the fact. In the midst of the States existing on our planet, each of them limited in space by pervious or impervious frontiers and exclusively occupied in organizing or accumulating earthly goods, there is a society with no definable frontier in space, older in time than all modern States, leading its own autonomous existence and professedly concerning itself solely with eternity and the roads that lead to it. Yet the clearly centralized government of this society has diplomatic relations with a large number of these States.

Further, the Church has cells in almost all the nations of the world. These are her dioceses and in the dioceses are the parishes. She has her own tribunals, her own special code of law, her own system of jurisprudence.

She imposes on those under her authority certain definite and clearly visible practices. Every Sunday they attend a place of corporate worship, they refuse to eat meat on Fridays and they fast several times a year. Marriage for them is indissoluble. Some of the members of this society adopt a way of life which separates them from the others, they wear a special dress and remain celibate. Some of them also accept the obligations of a common life, of poverty and obedience to a superior.

Faced with such a spectacle, the spectator who is that and nothing more grows angry, anxious or rejoices according to his temperament. Some openly admit that the Church gives them hope. With her powerful organization, her solid structure, her age-long experience, she is the bulwark, in their view, of all social order, and of "Christian civilization". These dubious supporters congratulate the Church on having adapted the message of Christ to the conventions and needs of the times, on having eliminated the poison from the *Magnificat*. Behind this bulwark, some hasten to put their money-bags in a safe place, others find shelter there for their fears, and others again for their terror of everything new.

To these groups might be added others, those for instance who are desperately anxious to see a revolution and who ask the Church to justify, bless and support the subversive activities of which they dream. But all these men are mistaken, whether they approve of or oppose the Church. They see and they will always see only the outward appearance of the Church. In short they will never see her as she is.

THE INVISIBLE CHURCH

At the other extreme are those Christians who look at the Church with the eye of faith. But they are in danger of making a similar mistake and it would be naïve to believe that they have all avoided falling victims to it.

Some are tempted to consider in the Church only her invisible and supernatural reality. Her visible and outward aspect is not attractive in all respects. Far from it. The Christian is disappointed in his brethren who are by no means all models of virtue, he is deceived in the Church's leaders who are not all geniuses nor even saints. Some are astonished at and scandalized by the vast machinery of what is called her administration, by the worldly noise and bustle made by the government of this huge body and by methods which remind them of secular States.

And so the Christian, in order to safeguard his faith in the Church, is, in a sense, prone to deny that her exterior and visible aspect is essential. He finds himself as it were forced to look beyond the earthly face which the Church turns to him, forced to brush appearances aside. After all, is not the Church rather to be found beyond our history, in the act of God which gives us faith and justifies us? Is not the Church of God within us, in the secret places of those souls who accept faith and justification? Let us be willing, say these Christians, to abandon the human, visible community to its wretchedness and pettiness, to its scandals, and let us fix our eyes solely upon the holy and indivisible Church, beyond this present time; let us look forward to its transcendent future. The Church is the object of our faith and not of our experience, even our religious experience. This Church is a thing to be hoped for, not a present reality. The Church exists as an ideal, not in history.

The spiritual attitude thus adumbrated is certainly found in Protestantism. It would be wrong to think that it does not also exist among Catholics as a tendency. Whatever the deep-seated intentions their defenders have in mind, such attitudes in no way do justice to the mystery of the Church.

THE CHURCH AND HER MYSTERY

What then is the mystery of the Church? The word must be understood in the original sense of *Musterion* as explained on several occasions by St Paul (1 Cor. 2. 7–8; Rom. 16. 25–7; Col. 1. 24–8; 2. 2–4; Ephes. 3. 3–12).

Hence "mystery" must not be watered down until it becomes only a hidden truth which the mind finds obscure. Mystery is an event produced by God's power and revealed by God in the very act of bringing it about. This event affects men and calls upon them to act. In fact, mystery is "Christ among you" (Col. 1. 24–8), an infinite event of which the Church is one facet.

In this sense and for this reason, the mystery of the Church consists in the interdependence, within her walls, of history and the eternity of God, of man and of God, of the visible and invisible. To use a more direct expression: the Church is the assembly of those who are baptized and inspired by supernatural faith in Jesus Christ. They recognize the authority of Peter, of the Apostles and their successors. And, *at the same time,* the Church is the instrument by means of which God in his mercy provides for the salvation of the whole human race. The mystery is the union of these two points of view. On the one hand, it is a human society, and on the other, it prolongs the existence of Christ.

St Gregory of Nyssa has expressed this mystery of the Church in a passage of great brilliance:

> The foundation of the Church is the creation of a new universe . . . In the Church, another man is formed in the image of him who created him. In her, is a new species of stars (the apostles), of whom it is said: "You are the light of the world." . . . And just as one who looks at the world he perceives with his senses and seizing that Wisdom which is manifested in the beauty of created beings, passes beyond visible things to those that are invisible, so too he who considers this new Cosmos which is the creation of the Church, sees in it him who is and who becomes all in all. Thus he directs his mind toward the incomprehensible God, taking it, as it were, by the hand and passing through and beyond both sensible objects and the objects of faith" (*In cant. canticorum*, 13, Migne, *Patrologia Graeca* 44, 1049; hereafter referred to as *P.G.*).

This is tantamount to saying that the Church *is* something very different from what she *appears to be*. She is not only the mirror in which shines the sun of justice (as St Gregory of Nyssa says—*In cant. canticorum*, 8, *P.G.* 44. 949), she is also God's dwelling-place.

Hence the Church is not only a human community, not only an object of historical experience, although she is both of these. The Church is a mystery of faith, although she is not only a mystery of faith.

The mystery lies in the fact that, throughout the ages and in every continent, the "little flock" becomes the mediator of grace for the whole human race. The mystery lies in the fact that every man has most certainly his part to play in the history of the Church's life; it lies in the fact that the whole enterprise will only succeed through the concerted effort of the human mass, for "we too are co-workers with God".

This then is the mystery in its original sense. It is a *truth* we could not have discovered if supernatural revelation had not intervened, a *reality* whose nature remains obscure to us even after Revelation, an *activity* in which we are all involved and called upon to play a part whose implications are beyond definition and in the supernatural order. It is from this standpoint that the Church is an object of faith, not under her human and historical aspects which are facets of experience, but in her inner supernatural nature, in so far, that is, as she is sanctified by the Spirit, shares in the holiness of God and becomes the reflection of his truth and the instrument of his saving love.

Yet since the mystery of the Church is inseparable from her human outward appearance, scandal lies in wait for man, for every man, for the unbeliever inevitably, but for the believer also. The Church is at one and the same time divine and human, great and abject. We find it difficult to accept these two aspects and to link them together. The second obscures the first. In a similar way, the Jews long ago saw the Son of God moving from one place to another, eating and drinking, and they were tempted to be scandalized. Many of them fell into this trap. But "Blessed is he whosoever shall not be scandalized in me" (Luke 7. 23).

CHAPTER I

THE MYSTERY OF THE CHURCH BEFORE HER FOUNDATION

The origin of the Church raises a problem. Where did this community come from? How is it to be explained? Is the explanation to be found solely on the human level? Is the Church the creation of history like the empire of the Incas and industrial civilizations? Or must we say, on the contrary, that the explanation is to be sought in the realm of the supernatural so that the Church can never be considered as a purely human phenomenon?

We must reply at once that the Church is not explained simply by intentions and acts of a purely historical character, but by an Event absolutely beyond the whole natural historical order which is yet inscribed upon it and changes its course, and this event is a decision of God's will. Of course, when we utter this truth, we immediately come up against the common opinion which holds that the Church's existence is no more than the consequence of sociological laws. According to this view, the Church emerged only because man must live in society if he wishes to survive biologically, intellectually, morally and religiously. This notion undoubtedly contains an element of truth, yet it must be pronounced radically incomplete, and altogether illusory, if it is supposed to be the whole truth.

The Church's origin is *a supernatural mystery* which has two different aspects. On the one hand, her origin lies outside time and hidden in God. It is the eternal thought in terms of which the Master of Time has decided to write the history of men and to lead it to its appointed end through Jesus Christ and his Church. God has *predestined* time as the vehicle of the Church.

On the other hand, the mystery of the Church came down into time and this even before the Church made her visible appearance in human history. During that period God directed the course of history in anticipation of the coming of the Church, and brought progressively to light symbols and rough outlines of the future Church in the course of human events and in a symbolical manner. The Church was the object of *prophecy*.

It will perhaps be objected that if prophecy works by means of symbols and rough outlines, then it scarcely deserves to be called "prophecy". It is true that if "prophecy" is taken to mean purely and simply "prediction", that is, "a forecast and complete description of a future, clearly defined event", then there can be no question of prophecy in this case. But the fact is that the prophecies of the Old Testament constitute a repeated, progressive forecast of God's will directing men's hopes and expectations towards a predetermined future, yet without giving any precise description of the end in view or a full-length representation of the event foretold. Since prophecy is defined in these terms it is only recognized as prophecy after the event. Hence the Jews who heard the prophets announce the triumphs of Israel at some time in the future could not know that their people prefigured the Church, although they were perfectly aware that their nation was preparing for the universal Kingdom of God. We, on the other hand, see the Church as God's people and so are able to recognize retrospectively in the outlines of the past the emergence of the Church above the Jewish horizon.

THE CHURCH AS PREDESTINED

Why does the Church exist? The only possible explanation is that she is the result of the sovereign decision of God who has destined her for this earth during a given period of time and in a determined area. No natural explanation of the Church is sufficient. Yet this reality, which cannot be explained historically, is at the centre of history. The Church is made up of men, she experiences the effects of events, she has some influence on these events, but she is not their product. St Paul long ago told the Christians of Ephesus that our community, gathered from the mass of humanity, is the result of an eternal plan. The Church which we form is not the result of chance, even providential chance:

> Blessed be that God, that Father of our Lord Jesus Christ, who has blessed us, in Christ, with every spiritual blessing, higher than heaven itself. *He has chosen us out, in Christ, before the foundation of the world,* to be saints, to be blameless in his sight, for love of him; *marking us out beforehand* (so his will decreed) to be his adopted children through Jesus Christ . . . to make known to us the hidden *purpose of his will.* It was his loving design, centred in Christ, to give history its fulfilment by resuming everything in him, all that is in heaven, all that is on earth, summed up in him. *In him it was our lot to be called, singled out beforehand to suit his purpose* (*for it is he who is at work everywhere, carrying out the designs of his will*); we were to manifest his glory, we who were the first to set our hope in Christ. (Ephes. 1. 3–12 *passim.*)

And so, while man thinks that he is controlling the world's progress, the Church is coming into existence, in God's secret plan, from the beginning until the end of time. The *Ecclesia* is God's project for man's time and the latter is only shaped into history thanks to the Church. This is the law of that time which is our own. Once this has been recognized, we must come down to the level of history as the historians understand it in order to identify the other aspects of the mystery. Thus we can see how God announces and realizes his plan in the concrete, how the prophecy which foretells the Church unrolls itself.

THE CHURCH AS PROPHESIED

In a sense that needs to be made clear, the Church existed in the Old Testament. The Fathers were convinced of this and they quite simply declared that the just men of the Old Testament already belonged to the Church.

The first Christians in the Apostolic Church expressed the same idea in a different way. They were conscious of being the true Israel, the true people of God, of continuing a very ancient history, as ancient in fact as that of Moses. St Paul, so keenly aware of Christianity as a new thing, nevertheless calls the assembly of the faithful the true Israel and the children of Christian truth the descendants of Abraham (Gal. 4. 28; Rom. 9. 6–13). This is why he finds no difficulty in declaring that Abraham is "the father of all of us" who are Christians (Rom. 4. 12–16). As St Gregory of Nyssa was later to write: "if all those who are pure in heart see God, then those who indeed see him are, and are rightly called, Israel."[1]

The fact that the Christians were aware that spiritually they were Jews is made clear by another phenomenon. The

[1] *In cant. canticorum,* 7; *P.G.* 44, 904.

word *laos* (people) formerly applied to Israel, the people of God, was now used of Christ's faithful. This is a minor point perhaps, yet it reveals the spontaneous certainty felt that a prophecy is fulfilled in the Church of Christ and that the true people has come into existence.[2] Though this fulfilment is achieved in the *Ecclesia*, a beginning had therefore been made in the past before Christ, before there were any Christians. The Church then existed even before she became visible, as St Gregory the Great saw when he wrote: "The Church, already in existence under the Old Law, longed and waited for Christ."[3]

But although the Church existed under the former dispensation, it was only in hope, in mere outline. Her presence there was like that of the oak tree in the acorn. Her growth was to be a long and exacting labour spread over many centuries. In the course of her development, there are certain particularly decisive moments.

God's chosen people, the Church in germ

The Church was prophesied from the day when a group of men was gathered together by an immediate intervention on God's part and in his name.[4] That this event should have taken place and have been directly the work of God Almighty, is certainly the most amazing fact in our history. For this group was a set of men just like so many others in their instincts and passions. It was made up of the descendants of those "seventy souls" who went into Egypt in the footsteps of Joseph, "increased and sprang up into multitudes, and growing exceedingly strong they filled the

[2] Strathmann, article "Laos", in Kittel, *Theologisches Wörterbuch zum neuen Testament,* p. 55.

[3] *In cant. canticorum,* Migne, *Patrologia Latina,* vol. 79, col. 538–9 (hereafter referred to as *P.L.* followed by volume and column number).

[4] It is however true that Christian thought has seen a "type" of the Church in events and persons before the time of the Exodus.

land" (Exod. 1. 5–7). Their subsequent history shows that this race was no less cruel, no less immoral than many others. It is just one race among others.

It is also a fact that this race, scattered throughout Egypt, was to regroup itself at the instigation of Moses. But it regrouped itself in the name of Yahweh and of the mission which Yahweh had conferred upon Moses. Then, still in the name of Yahweh, men, women and children left Egypt (Exod. 12. 38). They went forward into the desert, grumbling and rebelling; they grew closer to one another, and ultimately became a more or less homogeneous people, adoring the same God, marching towards the same goal, the Promised Land, and finally entering, once more in the name of Yahweh, into the land of Chanaan.

The regrouping of these Semite tribes was consecrated by the event of Sinai which gave it a transcendent and definitive sense. Indeed the meaning of this event was too much for these poor people. And that is understandable enough, for something tremendous had happened. God had chosen as his own special people this collection of intractable nomads and had linked it positively to himself as though he had genuine need of it. He revealed this fact in words which must have been far above the heads of the mass of the people: "You shall be my peculiar possession above all people: for all the earth is mine. And you shall be to me a priestly kingdom and a holy nation" (Exod. 19. 5–6).

Henceforth this people possessed a motto. But it was not of its own choice and its character was supernatural: "you shall be *my* people and I will be *your* God," proclaimed Yahweh.

The event on Sinai was decisive not because it was accompanied by thunder, lightning, a thick cloud and "the noise of the trumpet . . . exceeding loud" (Exod. 19. 16), but because it was essentially the inauguration of the

Covenant. It is this which is so amazing, it is here that the mystery lies, and at the same there is revealed for the first time the Church which was to come.

Everything is in the word "Covenant". It is a contract God made with these men and with no others. It is obvious that it occupied a unique place in the religious thought of the Hebrew people and its descendants. The frequent use of the word is sufficient evidence. The Hebrew *berith* (= Covenant) occurs 285 times; it is translated 275 times by the Greek word διαθήκη. The meaning attached to it is equally remarkable. For every Hebrew, the Covenant was an act that could not have been foreseen. It could only have been initiated by God. He chose this people and enlisted it in his service in a special manner, and in return he bound himself, so to speak, to this nation. The word "Covenant" does not therefore proclaim that all peoples belong to God. On the contrary, it means that God has turned towards this section of mankind, has attached it to himself, has "become converted" to it in the name of his own fidelity, because he has willed that this should be so (Deut. 7. 6). But it also means a direct entry into possession so that this race becomes "Yahweh's portion", his inherited share of the earth, his property in this world, as though the rest of the universe did not belong to him when compared with this special piece of property (Deut. 32. 9). The Covenant is one of mercy, yet at the same time, it is a legal relationship and creates mutual obligations.

From the time of Sinai onwards, the Hebrews therefore deserved the title of the people of God. There was no longer even any need to talk explicitly of its belonging to God. The word "people" was sufficient to indicate "the people of God". It was this that distinguished Israel from all the others who were only "nations".[5]

[5] Strathmann, *op. cit.*, pp. 32, 35. Cf. Menoud, article "Église", in Von Allmen, *Vocabulaire biblique,* p. 83 (both authors are Protestants).

They are indeed a strange people. As a people, they owe to God alone their existence, constitution and country (Deut. 4. 34–8; 32. 6–11; 33. 29). Their vocation consists in keeping themselves for God alone. They will go forward into the future even though they are forbidden to marry the daughters of neighbouring nations or to contract alliances with these same nations (Deut. 7. 1–4). Their political programme, the only one allowed to them, is to believe in Yahweh and not on any account to model their conduct on the wisdom of men. It is under these conditions that they deserve to be called by God "my son, my first-born" (Exod. 4. 22).

Israel belonged so exclusively to God that the prophet Samuel refused permission for the election of a king "to judge us, as all nations have" (1 Kings 8. 5). To have done this would have been to infringe the prerogative of God who alone was their king "for they have not rejected thee, but me, that I should not reign over them" (1 Kings 8. 7). Although ultimately they were permitted to have a king, yet God maintained his exclusive rule by choosing the man who should be given this power (1 Kings 10. 24; 2 Kings 7. 8) and by exercising sovereign control over the royal line until the end of time (2 Kings 7. 12–16; Jer. 23. 5–6; 33. 14; Ezech. 33. 24–31; 37. 24–8). Although it was given earthly rulers, God's people did not therefore receive a new prince. If ever the rulers and the ruled forgot this, the prophets, at times in violent terms, reminded the kings that their role was a ministry and a subordinate one (3 Kings 18 and 19; Osee 13. 4–11; Isaias 43. 15; 44. 6).

Thus the Jewish people bore a stamp which was unique. Israel was the property of God. She only possessed land, country, kings and her own existence by virtue of a special decree of God in her favour. Whereas the "nations" possessed their gods, Israel was the possession of her God who is the one sole Master of the world.

This surely reminds us of the "little flock" which the Son of God gathered to himself at a much later date. It is he, the Son of God, who is responsible for the gathering together of the flock, and it belongs to him. When he speaks of what he has just done, he uses the words: "My 'assembly', my Church". He it is who appoints its leaders. This took place also on a mountain but quietly, for the Word of God became true man (cf. Luke 6. 12–16). Finally, these Twelve men will be led by the Son of God far from the beaten track of mankind, far from the things that interest men. They will live in poverty so that they may care for only one thing: "Thy Kingdom come, thy will be done on earth as it is in heaven." Jesus is the new Moses, but he is greater than Moses.

The people's witness as a figure of the Church

Israel's specific characteristics become even more apparent if we consider the mission which she was given. Her mission was not merely to exist, to rule, to play a part on the political stage. Above all else, it was to bear witness to the fact that God had a plan for the world and that this plan was accomplished in and also through Israel. This plan was nothing less than the universal Kingdom of Yahweh. To all this Israel was to bear witness. Her very definition was "people of the testimony": "Behold I have given you for a witness to the people" (Isaias 55. 4).

Israel then is the servant of the reign of Yahweh. The only reason for Jerusalem's existence is that she may be the place from which God's plan originates and in which it is fulfilled:

> For the law shall go forth out of Sion, and the word of the Lord out of Jerusalem (Micheas 4. 2; Isaias 2. 2–4). But the Lord shall arise upon thee (Jerusalem), and his glory

shall be seen upon thee. And the gentiles shall walk in thy light, and kings in the brightness of thy rising. (Isaias 60. 2–3.)

Israel is also God's witness as the instrument through which Yahweh's Reign is established, not for the sake of the pagan nations, as in the passages just quoted, but in opposition to them (Isaias 10. 17). And Israel is still more the people of the testimony and in a far nobler fashion, because she is concerned with the glory of God and confesses that she is responsible for it before the whole world. The following beautiful prayer is an instance of this: "That they may know thee, as we also have known thee, that there is no God beside thee, O Lord . . . let all know that dwell upon the earth, that thou art God the beholder of all ages" (Ecclus. 36. 5–19).

The people of the testimony is responsible for the truth. They are to declare it to the others but first and foremost they are to preserve it themselves. And they are well aware of what this primordial truth is. It was given to them in a most solemn manner: "Thou shalt not have strange gods before me" (Exod. 20. 3–23). If, then, the people of the testimony prevaricates and ceases to bear witness, it loses the whole reason for its existence, there is nothing left for it to do but to perish. Hence the apostasy which broke out during the absence of Moses, the worship of the golden calf, demanded a punishment which already foreshadowed the disappearance of the people for "there were slain that day about three and twenty thousand men" (Exod. 32. 28). There are other equally terrible examples. To the latter is linked a perfectly clear teaching: "Beware lest perhaps your heart be deceived . . . and the Lord being angry shut up heaven . . . and you perish quickly from the excellent land, which the Lord will give you" (Deut. 11. 16–17). These are the words of Moses. But others will repeat them again and again. All the prophets were very eloquent on this subject, Amos (2. 4–16), Isaias (5. 8–30), Jeremias (1. 15–17) and Ezechiel (33. 23–9).

In a word, the mission of God's people is strictly religious, although Israel had to lead a political existence involved in international events. But here again they were unique. They were aware of it too, although they never completely grasped how unique they were to be.

The unfolding of prophecy

Thus the prophetic foreshadowing of the Church continued. To the characteristics we have just mentioned, others were added and they are astonishing. For prophecy has a positive and negative aspect. The negative aspect is the temporal failure of Israel. Its positive aspect is the declaration that even in its failures Israel will nevertheless continue to exist and that its future is unlimited.

Failure

We must trace briefly the sequence of Israel's ordeals if we are to understand how they were transcended. The failure is both that of the nation and, or so it would appear, of God's plan. As "Yahweh's portion" and his witness, the nation had received an immense and crushing mission. It was to prove unequal to its vocation and it fell under the weight of so great an honour.

The apostasy at Sinai at the very moment of the nation's election and of the Covenant, is symptomatic and was to be followed by many others. Every event was to lead to apostasy: the establishment of the nation in the land of Chanaan among the idol-worshipping tribes, contacts with the great peoples of the Orient. Idolatry was never to cease completely in the chosen people whether under the Judges or the Kings. Ecclesiasticus, viewing the past history of the royal house, had sadly to declare: "Except David, and Ezechias, and Josias, all committed sin" (49. 5).

Israel was taught that, since it was a consecrated nation, it could put its trust only in one God. The story of the Exodus was constantly repeated as a proof and an illustration of this strictly religious destiny. Yet Israel could never make up its mind to be simply the people of God. The tribes demanded a king because they wanted to organize their own security and their own greatness, as though God might break faith with them. This was their sin, and the failure of the Covenant lay in this also, as all of them well knew: "We have added to all our sins this evil," they said, "to ask for a king" (1 Kings 12. 19). Later, they were to consider that the Covenant with God was a sorry means of defence against powerful neighbours with their chariots and horses. And so, to the increasing indignation of the prophets, they looked elsewhere (Isaias 7. 1–9; 30. 1–7; cf. 22. 8–12). Worship itself was reduced to the status of a mere guarantee against misfortune (Isaias 1. 11–18; Amos 5. 21–7). In short, Israel did not wish to be a people apart to the extent prescribed by Yahweh when he declared: "You shall be holy, because I am holy" (Lev. 11. 46). In spite of all reprimands, Israel hesitated to put all its trust in the one and only "Rock" (Ps. 18. 32; Deut. 32. 3; Isaias 44. 8; 45. 21). In short, Israel did not succeed in being what it was intended to be when God gathered it together, namely the people of faith, the people of Yahweh.

Hence it was only with great difficulty that it remained the people of the Covenant. The Covenant itself was finally broken, it might seem, by repeated infidelity. "Yes," declared Yahweh, "I will go and return to my place" (Osee 5. 15), "they have transgressed the covenant, there have they dealt treacherously against me" (Osee 6. 7). The prophets continually repeated that the Covenant had been wilfully torn up and made void by the people (Isaias 24. 5). The prophets did not scruple to exasperate their hearers by using very graphic images, that of adultery for instance, and from the eighth century onwards they declared that the Covenant was in process of dissolution because of Israel's sins (Osee 1. 9; 2. 5; Jer. 11. 10; 31. 32; Ezech. 16. 59; 44. 7).

With the appearance of the Deutero-Isaias in the sixth century we have the impression that the time of the Mosaic Covenant was over. No memory of it remained, so it would seem, no foundation on which to rebuild (Isaias 54. 10; 55. 3; 61. 8 *et seq.*).

Israel then is about to perish. This is the natural fulfilment of the threatening prophecy in the book of Leviticus (26. 14). Deuteronomy repeats it (28. 15 *et seq.*) and sums up the thought common to the earlier prophets: God will not hold back his just anger. Since in practice the people have apostasized, the contract entered into on Sinai is annulled. Since the nation refuses its original function, it can and it must disappear.

This was in fact what happened. In spite of a few temporary reforms, the decadence of the twelve tribes was to continue increasingly. After Solomon's ephemeral glory came the schism of the Northern tribes (*c.* 931), then the destruction of the Northern Kingdom (721) and that of the Kingdom of Juda (587). This was followed by the exile. When it was over, one form of servitude succeeded another until the ruin of Jerusalem (70 A.D.) and the dispersal of the Jewish people over the face of the earth.

The transcending of failure

It was both in and because of this long story of failure that the prophetic foreshadowing of the Church continued. In fact, it is in opposition and contrast to the dissolution of the people of the Covenant that the pattern of the future began to take shape. We need only recall one or two of the more important occasions to make this point clear.

Between the eighth and the fourth centuries, the prophets

were constantly foretelling the destruction of the chosen people, yet they passed directly and without any transition to the assurance that this same people would begin afresh and would last for ever. Thus, while they predicted the annihilation of Israel, they were equally insistent that the prophecy of Nathan to David would be fulfilled: "And thy house shall be faithful, and thy kingdom for ever before thy face" (2 Kings 7. 16).

Their utterances also explained how the people, doomed to destruction as it was, would yet continue to exist. They used the images of the past or the present to prophesy the future, and they declared that the people of God, divided by the schism of 931, would be reunited, that its scattered sections, Israel and Juda, would be brought together again (Osee 2. 2–3; Ezech. 37. 15–19), that David would return, that Jerusalem was to be invincible and would for ever give its light (Isaias 54. 11–15; 60. 19–20; Ezech. 40 to 48), that God's Reign would be finally established among the people and that through the latter's agency the Kingdom of Yahweh would be inaugurated over the whole world (Isaias 45. 23–5; cf. 52. 7; 60. 14–16; Jer. 33. 9).

Thus the victory which God alone would win would cause the people of God to triumph and to receive a perpetual guarantee against death. The prophets promised an Israel that would never perish, just as the Church was to receive from Christ the same assurance that it would endure for ever.

But, we may ask, is it really Israel that is described in such splendid terms? Is there any continuity between the Israel of the present and the Israel to come? There can be no doubt about the answer. It was the people at the time, or their descendants at least, who were to be the people of God in the future. Certainly the prophets foretold that the nation of their day would be diminished and lose considerable sections of its people. Israel was to become no more than "a remnant".[6] But already in the eighth century Amos declared that such a remnant would remain (3. 12; 5. 15).

Israel was to be renewed spiritually. At a future but unspecified date a "New Covenant" was to be entered into, since the first had proved to be unworkable. The New Covenant would be eternal (Isaias 53. 3; Jer. 31. 31–4; Ezech. 37. 26). It was to inaugurate the last and definitive epoch in human history. An event of great importance would then take place. The Covenant and the Law would no longer be inscribed on tablets of stone as on Sinai, but on the hearts of men and by the Spirit of God. Henceforth justice in its spiritual sense would dwell among the generations of the future:

> I will give my law in their bowels, and I will write it in their heart (Jer. 31. 33). I will pour out my spirit upon all flesh . . . upon my servants and handmaids in those days I will pour forth my spirit . . . every one that shall call upon the name of the Lord shall be saved: for in mount Sion, and in Jerusalem shall be salvation (Joel 2. 28–32).

Hence the people of the future was to be a nation of just men: "They shall not hurt, nor shall they kill in all my holy mountain, for the earth is filled with the knowledge of the Lord, as the covering waters of the sea" (Isaias 12. 9). Then Israel would be truly God's people, the flock led by the Good Shepherd, Yahweh himself: "Behold I myself will seek my sheep, and will visit them" (Ezech. 34. 11–16). Then Israel would be given the rank of the nation who is the Bride of the Lord: "Thy creator is thy bridegroom" (Isaias 54. 5).

This glorious future is prophesied with other images

[6] The name "Israel" which was first used of the Northern Kingdom in contrast with the Kingdom of the South (Juda), later indicated the "remnant" that remained faithful to God. The word therefore acquired a religious sense.

also. Israel is described as a city and a temple at one and the same time and its builder is Yahweh (Isaias 54. 11–12). Peace shall give judgement therein and justice shall govern; the gates shall be called "Praise" and the walls "Salvation" (Isaias 60. 17–18). This city deserves titles which are supernatural in character: "Thou shalt be called the city of the just" (Isaias 1. 26), "the city of the Lord, the Sion of the holy One of Israel" (60. 14), or, as Ezechiel says, "and the name of the city from that day, The Lord is there" (48. 35). Thus the people of the future is to be God's people in a more excellent sense, for it will be the people of the divine Presence.

Such characteristics obviously and infinitely transcend the "fleshly" Israel, entangled in its sins, its self-seeking, its unbelief. The prerogatives in question have the effect of transfiguring the earthly Israel, which was limited to the members of one race alone. If justice is the very pattern of the future Israel, it is surely essential that all the just men in the world should be its members and be part of the people of God. This point of view was already present in the revelation made to Abraham (Gen. 12. 1 *et seq.*); it was restated and developed by the prophets. All men are called to be saved, even those who live in "the furthest part of the earth" (Isaias 49. 6). More exactly, the gate of the city will not be closed to the stranger who is faithful to the true God, it will not be closed to the eunuch, and God adds: "I will bring them into my holy mount, and will make them joyful in my house of prayer; their holocausts, and their victims shall please me upon my altar; for my house shall be called the house of prayer, for all nations" (Isaias 56. 3–7). Although equality between all men is not yet proclaimed—Jesus Christ will be the first to do this—yet it is clearly stated that salvation is offered to all.

These characteristics could not be applied to the Israel known to the authors of the sacred books. Yet it is indeed this people and its destiny which they were describing. But gone are the narrow-mindedness, the legalistic formalism and "the stiff neck". Another world arises, spiritual, boundless and guaranteed against all disintegration and regression. This is surely a figure of the Church on earth, universal and indefectible.

At the same time this picture suggests the Church triumphant, the Church beyond time and this earth. It shows us a world in which men no longer do evil, in which pain, sorrow and death have passed away. Such prophecies could only be fulfilled in God's eternity and not in any historical future. This is undeniable.

Thus the Jerusalem of the future seems to be neither wholly heavenly nor wholly earthly. Here again there is surely a foreshadowing of the Church which leads its life on the earth but is only complete in God and in eternity. Then she will possess "foundations with sapphires . . . bulwarks of jasper, gates of graven stones, and . . . borders of desirable stones" (Isaias 54. 11–12). Yahweh will give her light when "the days of thy mourning shall be ended" (Isaias 60. 20, cf. 54. 11–12). These two horizons, one in eternity, the other in time, are superimposed, and one is the prolongation of the other. The historical, terrestrial nation is a figure of another historical and terrestrial people, the people of the saints who are admitted to the vision of God.

In spite of the obscurity inherent in this twofold prospect, one thing is clear; the future that is foretold will only come about after a time of crisis which will be Israel's tragedy. There will be a period of calamity, of national upheavals, nationwide disasters, the destruction of Jerusalem and of the Temple, slavery and exile. These are absolutely essential conditions if a "remnant" faithful to and worthy of God's plan is to be formed and is to return.

If we follow the teaching about this "remnant" in the

prophecies of Isaias, we shall see that the "it" is identified with a mysterious person, "the Servant of Yahweh".[7] He is both the "remnant" as a group and as an individual whose mission is to save Israel and all mankind. And still more significant is the fact that the Kingdom of Yahweh is centred on this person. He is the chosen one of God (Isaias 42. 1–6), the "remnant", the Covenant of the people (Isaias 49. 8), the just man (Isaias 42. 1; 50. 4–5).

The Servant of Yahweh is therefore presented as the true Israel, faithful to the Covenant, and the instrument of universal salvation. But the "remnant" is very reduced indeed since it is composed of one man alone. And the crisis is formally predicted for the Servant also, and in quite concrete terms. He will be "despised and the most abject of men, a man of sorrows, and acquainted with infirmity" (Isaias 53. 3).

In and through this utter anguish, the mission formerly entrusted to the whole nation, and now declared to be that of the Servant, will be fulfilled. He will be the instrument through which the reign of Yahweh will be brought about (Isaias 49. 6–7). By offering his life in expiation, "he shall see a long-lived seed and the will of the Lord shall be prosperous in his hand . . . by his knowledge shall this my just servant justify many, and he shall bear their iniquities" (Isaias 53. 10–11).

Thus, beginning with the "remnant" of Israel summed up in the Servant, and because of it, God's Reign will spread afar and will be successfully established. "Therefore will I distribute to him very many", says the prophecy

[7] It is not possible here nor is it necessary to go into the details of a problem which has caused much ink to flow. The texts represent the Servant of Yahweh sometimes as a collectivity and sometimes as an individual. The meaning of the passages in question cannot be gainsaid, although the association of collective and individual characteristics in relation to one and the same being baffles the Western mind.

(Isaias 53. 12). The existence of the Servant is therefore in itself the promise of an unbounded fertility, of a renewal of life through death. What is prophesied is the triumph of the Cross, and this triumph will mean a universe of men redeemed by the Cross.

So the Servant of Yahweh is none other than Christ. Israel, according to God's plan, was to end in him, to disappear in him as a race and an instrument of salvation. And it would rise anew in him as the people of the New Covenant, recruited in the name of justice to carry universal salvation to the ends of the earth.

We are now in a position to attempt a rapid survey of the prophecies as a whole. The prophets spoke to the historical Israel in an attempt to convert it. Hence they were always ahead of the people, indicating to it what it ought to be. Their words threw up beyond the existing Israel the picture of a nobler Israel and this picture was projected on to a future which God would order.

At the historical level, the Jewish people failed again and again, and this painful process, interpreted as it was by the prophets and understood by the humble, teaches the necessity of renouncing all worldly aims, the need to abandon human ambitions, the essential requirement of a faith which is absolute. Only a small number of men would assimilate these truths, only the "remnant". But if left to itself, the "remnant" would not have been able to renew the nation, to revivify it, to change its heart. The "remnant" was to become smaller still and eventually to be summed up in Christ. He is the effectual instrument of salvation, he is the "Servant of Yahweh". And only he could be this instrument and this Servant since he is the Word of God in person.

It was now possible for Israel to begin a new growth from the stem of Jesse, from this son of David. It could now increase and multiply and fill the whole earth. Now began the faithful Israel, the universal Israel, the Israel whom God has loved from all eternity, and whose gates he opens to every man who hungers and thirsts after justice. This Israel is the holy "assembly" which we call the universal Church.

But first the Cross had to stand on Golgotha.

CONCLUSION

The mystery of the Church is therefore at work even before the word "Church" itself has been uttered. This mystery is beyond time not only in the divine Mind which decreed the existence of the Church from all eternity, but also in the supernatural providence which constantly keeps watch over the Church's gradual emergence. And this is the mystery of *divine prevenience*.

The mystery of the Church has also been present in time since the beginning of the world. It is on her behalf that the Master of History has intervened in its processes. The Church, then, is to appear in God's good time, and all creatures through her are to be brought together under one single Head, Christ Jesus. Until this time comes and in order that it may come, God arouses in the hearts of the best among his people the desire and the hope of his reign. To some he also suggests the outlines of what is to come in the shape of magnified images of their present experience. The mystery of the Church is the mystery of the Divine Presence in the days of Israel. During that time God wrote on the page of human freedom a special story, composed of the joy and suffering of men in their lives and in their deaths. But in this story, in itself so like many others and so unspectacular, we find not only the hopes and fears of men, but also God's plan of mercy and transfiguration.

CHAPTER II

THE MYSTERY OF THE CHURCH AT THE TIME OF HER BIRTH

We have accompanied the Jewish people down the course of the centuries, and have now reached the period at which the historians place the time of the Church's birth. It was then that she appeared in the light of day and left behind the secret of her prehistory. Surely then she passed from mystery to the realm of experience and became the Church in fact, a simple, verifiable reality like all things that have a historical existence. The mystery of the Church must cease in Palestine in the first century of our era.

What have Christians to say about this? Nobody doubts that the birth of the Church is a historical fact, verifiable by historical methods. All that Jesus of Nazareth did when he founded the Church has long since been catalogued and labelled. His words and deeds have been dated, and all their details commented upon and discussed. The appearance of the Church is, for historians, a fact of the same type as the appearance of any human society.

Catholic theologians are not likely to deny this, nor will they prevent us from giving this point of view a privileged position, since they themselves (with some exceptions) place on the process of the Church's juridical institution predominant and all but exclusive emphasis. They have no option, of course, yet to judge from what they say, we might well end up by believing that the founding of the Church was an act like so many others, like a decision taken by any individual who has made up his mind to found a sports club, a friendly society, a society to encourage scientific research and so forth. The birth of the Church, therefore, would seem to be merely a matter of obtaining "a writ from the sheriff's officer" and of finding the best method of putting it into operation.

Such being the case, it is understandable that some Christians, Protestants, for instance, and others also, should be disinclined to adopt an idea which, in their opinion, ignores the meaning of Revelation. They prefer to state (and here they in their turn take too one-sided a view) that the birth of the Church is an "event" in the sphere of grace, purely and simply. It is an invisible mystery and it is much more important to believe by faith that this mystery exists and is transcendent than to discover whether and how it is a fact of history. If pressed a little, these Christians would say that the institution of the Church, in the juridical sense dear to Roman Catholics, is far too trivial a reality to account for the birth of the Church in all the fullness of its truth.

Fortunately it is not necessary to choose between these points of view, on the assumption that they are contradictory. The birth of the Church is both an act of *institution,* an act which gives the Church her visible, verifiable and historical law, and at the same time a *supernatural event*—and so invisible and transcending history. God has willed that these two aspects of one and the same reality should not be separable but essentially interdependent.

The birth of the Church is a mystery of both faith and history. It is a fact which transcends time and the men who act upon its stage. Yet this fact is present in history under visible outward forms and in human acts. The

Roman Catechism long ago declared that the foundation of the Church is a mystery which is truly recognized only by faith, although even a Turk or a Jew may see something of what the Church is (Part I, chapter 10, No. 17 and No. 18). And we may add today, "even the unbeliever". It is interesting to note that Karl Barth, a Protestant, quotes this passage with approval (*Kirchliche Dogmatik* (1953), IV, 1, pp. 735–6).

We shall insist upon the visible and juridical aspects of the founding of the Church, that is, her "institution". At the same time we shall not forget the divine invisible operation, that is, the charismatic event.[1] These two elements are interdependent and the mystery of the Church's birth lies in their interdependence.

THE FOUNDATION OF THE CHURCH AND THE MYSTERY OF CHRIST

In the religious history of mankind, the foundation of the Church is not an episode on a par with others. It is linked with the historical Christ and, as a moment's thought will reveal, it also depends upon the total mystery, that is, Christ in all his fullness (Col. 1. 25 *et seq.*). To realize this, we must use the eye of faith. The foundation of the Church, in fact, takes place throughout the historical existence of our Lord, and in the Man-God himself both before and after his Resurrection. In some respects, it is continued until the end of time. The following pages will try to demonstrate these facts.

[1] The word "institution" is used by Catholic theologians to indicate the juridical, organizational aspect of the words of Jesus about the Church. The term "event" in the sense of divine grace, is used fairly frequently by Protestants today. Cf. for example, the title of J. L. Leuba's book *L'Institution et l'événement,* which has done much to give currency to this terminology even among Catholics.

Christ himself invites us to think of the constitution of the Church as a mystery unfolding itself over a period of time. At Caesarea after Peter's confession: "Thou art the Christ, the Son of the living God", Jesus declared: "I will build my Church." He spoke in the future tense. Although he had appointed Peter as head, and although he had already gathered around him his twelve first disciples, he did not consider that his Church was already built. He still referred to the future when he declared that Peter would receive the keys of the Kingdom of Heaven, and the power to bind and to loose (Matt. 16. 18–19). Again, he was looking to a future time when he conferred this same power of binding and loosing upon the Twelve (Matt. 18. 18). But at the moment when these words were pronounced, it was not clear when that time would come.

After the Last Supper when Christ had celebrated the Eucharist with the apostles, he spoke to them again in prophetic terms of a future event, the coming of the Holy Spirit (John 14. 16). And the Holy Spirit's mission directly concerns the Church, for it is he who is responsible for preserving the truth, for implanting it in the souls of the members of the Church (John 16. 13; 14. 20–26), and for maintaining the unity of the body of believers in Jesus Christ (John 14. 20). Thus Christ was suggesting that the foundation of the Church was to continue after his death since the Holy Spirit could only come when our Lord had left his followers.

THE FIRST STAGE OF THE CHURCH'S FOUNDATION BEFORE THE RESURRECTION

The Church was willed by Christ.[2] But if we are to appreciate the breadth and depth of his intentions, we

[2] Agreement on this point between Christians is more widespread today than at the beginning of the nineteenth century. Cf. F. M. Braun, *Nouveaux aspects du problème de l'Église,* 1942.

should do well to take up our position at the point where we can survey the whole mystery in both its human and its divine dimensions. And this vantage point is the Last Supper. This is because Christ, during the Last Supper, explained the ultimate meaning of his mission, of his life and death, and cast a clear light on the allusions and declarations which he had made on previous occasions.

On the Thursday evening (according to the traditional chronology), Jesus' "hour" had come, and he gathered his twelve companions around him for the last meal before his arrest and death. The occasion was unique. It was to be the fulfilment of the prophecies about the Kingdom of God and the Church. In these few hours, the "institution" was to be summed up in one act and the "event" which gave the institution its enduring efficacy was to take place.

The intention which had inspired our Lord from the beginning of his ministry now took on its exact meaning. The Kingdom of God was to be instituted, and it would be for ever linked with the mystery of Christ the Saviour and with the fact that its destinies were entrusted to the Twelve and their successors. The Old Testament seers had been haunted by the prospect of this advent of God's Kingdom and had represented it under the image of a heavenly banquet (Isaias 15. 16 *et seq.*). Christ took over this image (Matt. 8. 11; 22. 14 *et seq.*). He went much further, for on that particular evening, he anticipated the banquet of the Last Day with the bread and the wine on the table in the Upper Room, and he promised that the hope of the Kingdom would be infallibly fulfilled: "I have longed and longed to share this paschal meal with you before my passion; I tell you, I shall not eat it again, till it finds its fulfilment in the kingdom of God; . . . I tell you, I shall not drink of the fruit of the vine again, till the kingdom of God has come" (Luke 22. 16, 18).

Christ's intention

What did Christ understand by the Kingdom of God of which he spoke during these last hours, and how did he envisage its accomplishment?

If we are to answer these questions, we must go back to the three years which preceded the Last Supper. They prepared and outlined the foundation of the Church which was to take place during the course of this evening. Our Lord's purpose had been revealed on many occasions. He had come not only to teach the Good News, but to establish the true people and to lead the history of mankind to its appointed end through the agency of the people of the Covenant. And this is precisely what is meant by accomplishing the Kingdom of God.

During the Last Supper, Christ took up the expression "Kingdom of God" and reawakened in those at table with him thoughts and desires with which they were very familiar. He used images of surpassing grandeur: the Lord Yahweh would one day manifest his power to all the nations of the earth and would make himself known as the one and only Lord, as the one and only Master of Time, as the one and only King of all peoples. The Kingdom of God would know no bounds; its dimensions would extend to the whole earth, since God is Master of all men. It goes without saying, as the Scriptures repeat over and over again, that the advent of God's Reign could not take place except through Israel as its instrument. The apostles certainly had no doubts of it.

To prophesy the coming of the Kingdom of God was to prophesy by the same token the last period of history, the period in which the existence of Israel would no longer be called into question, in which the people of God would be re-established and would no longer have to fear death and the enemies who hitherto had led it astray in so melancholy a fashion. Once established, the Kingdom of God would never perish, it would be the final epoch of the world, it would be the Kingdom of the last days (Matt. 25. 31–46). And the Kingdom of God could not be thought of except as achieved through the agency of a people consecrated to God, an instrument of God, a mediator of universal salvation. And this people was obviously Israel. Jesus was implying that Israel would endure forever.

But certain points which he made were new, and then his hearers ceased to agree with him. He insisted that God's people would no longer be a political or racial entity (Mark 12. 17). How could it be, since the Kingdom of God is not? (John 18. 33). Entry into this Kingdom is therefore not by right of birth. The Kingdom is a spiritual world whose charter, which is also spiritual, is the Sermon on the Mount. Its values are those of the Beatitudes and of interior justice (Matt. 5. 1 *et seq.*; cf. Mark 10. 14–15). Hence the Kingdom of God can no longer be the privilege of one nation to the exclusion of another. In order to belong to this Kingdom, it is necessary and sufficient to make one's way of life the Beatitudes, to follow Christ wherever he may go (Matt. 16. 24–5), after being joined to him and to the Kingdom through baptism (John 3. 5; Mark 16. 16).

The only conditions for the new right of citizenship were justice and obedience to the leaders of the people (Matt. 16. 19; 18. 16). Hence also, the Kingdom of God was universal by right. By right also, equality was to exist between all its members. This was new. Nor was this the only example. The Jews thought that the Kingdom of God would come on earth. Doubtless, the grandiose images used by the prophets to describe the coming of the Kingdom must have puzzled them (see Isaias 11. 6–9; 25. 6–8; 60. 18–22) and led them to wonder in what place the Kingdom of God would be established. Would it be on earth? Would it be beyond present history and our world?

In actual fact, the Jews as a whole had thought only of an accomplishment on this earth. But Jesus had spoken and he had said that the Kingdom of God would come on earth, but at the same time that it would be accomplished beyond and above our history, in the presence of God, on that day when every man would receive his final reward or punishment according to his merits or demerits (Matt. 25. 31–46; cf. 13. 36–43).

One question remains to be answered: "Will Israel still have an exclusive part to play in the coming of the Kingdom? All Christ's hearers believed that it would and refused to give up their opinion. The prophecies which Christ claimed to fulfil clearly taught that Israel would continue to exist indefinitely. However, Christ explicitly stated that the privilege of the Jews had been abolished because of their acts of infidelity: "The kingdom of God will be taken away from you, and given to a people which yields the revenues that belong to it" (Matt. 21. 43; cf. 8. 11–12; 21. 34–6; 22. 1–14; cf. Luke 13. 6–9; 14. 15–24). There is a paradox here and its elements seem impossible to reconcile. The paradox is all the more provoking in that Christ declared himself to be the Messias, that is the King of Israel.

He no doubt did so from a very special point of view when he gave himself the title of "Son of Man", but that he made this claim cannot be denied. Elsewhere, Christ describes the Kingdom of the Son of Man and its inhabitants (Matt. 13. 41). Elsewhere again, he speaks of "his kingdom" (Matt. 16. 28; John 18. 36). Jesus is therefore the King of the Kingdom of God. He is also King of Israel. He accepts this title which is given to him by simple folk and he allows them to recall the fact of his Davidic origin.

Thus, in the person of Christ, Israel and the Kingdom of God seem to be exactly identical. But how then could

Christ declare at the same time that the Kingdom of God would be taken from Israel and given to another people?

The act of foundation

Christ, it would seem, was speaking in riddles. He himself declared that he was proclaiming the "secret of the Kingdom of Heaven". This secret, which he had already explained during the years of his public ministry, became clearer still during the Last Supper. It was then in fact that the establishment of the new Israel issuing from the old became apparent; it was then that the new Israel revealed itself as distinct from the former "people" of which nevertheless it was a continuation.

The Twelve in the Upper Room were not chance guests. They are the Twelve whom Christ had chosen "to be his companions" (Mark 3. 14). It is not they who had chosen their Master (John 15. 16), he had called them and, on this particular evening, they had been brought together once again. The Master had given these simple men a mission, they were to represent him personally (*shaliah*): "He who gives you welcome, gives me welcome too" (Matt. 10. 40; John 13. 20), "He who listens to you, listens to me" (Luke 10. 16). Whether or not they had understood it from the beginning, the twelve companions had become official persons in the order that was being established. The mother of the two sons of Zebedee at least had clearly grasped the fact (Matt. 20. 20).

Twelve men had been chosen and they had become "the Twelve" just as there were twelve tribes in Israel. On this particular evening they were gathered together as the representatives of the tribes, whose "remnant" they were. They also symbolized the people to come, they were its beginning according to Christ's will and through them the coming of the Kingdom of God was to be achieved. Although they were only a "little flock", yet it was to them that God had decided to entrust the care of the whole Kingdom (Luke 12. 32). In their midst was the King of peace, the Son of Man, the son of David, who had gathered them together. They were the official assembly of the people to be. That is why Jesus had named it in advance by using the word which had formerly indicated the official assembly of Israel in the desert (Deut. 9. 10). He had called it "my *Ecclesia*" (Matt. 16. 18; cf. 18. 17). Here, then, was the assembly of the new Israel, of which the true Messias, Jesus, is forever king.

The *Ecclesia* was gathered around the table and its members were about to eat the Pasch together. As long ago in Egypt the first Pasch had been the starting-point of the institution of the chosen people, so now too it was the decisive moment in the establishment of the new people, which thus succeeds the former Israel—*nova et vetera.*

They had met for a meal. In all the world's civilizations, the meal has a special meaning when taken in common. It signifies intimacy and familiarity, and it produces them. It is the ratification of the beginnings of a fellowship, it authorizes friendship and establishes a communion. On this particular evening, with Jesus in the centre, the meal had this precise meaning. The bond which bound them together as the *Ecclesia* was their love for our Lord and the friendship that linked them all to one another. It was no mere chance that Christ himself repeated his teaching on charity after the meal and in terms of great urgency (John 13. 33–6; 15. 1–7; 17. 21–6). Paul understood the reason perfectly when he wrote: "the one bread makes us one body" (1 Cor. 10. 17), one single family.

This meal marked the end of an epoch and at the same time the beginning of another. John's account contains a solemn introduction to the meal. Jesus was about to die. Yet the importance of the occasion was not determined solely by the imminence of his death but also by the events that were inseparable from it. An era was coming to its close. "I shall never eat this Pasch (of the Old Law) again", said Christ. The Mosaic Covenant was over and done with, yet its fulfilment was about to take place (". . . till it finds its fulfilment in the kingdom of God", Luke 22. 16). A whole world was on the point of disappearing, for Christ was about to die: "I shall not drink of the fruit of the vine again." With Christ, the Old Law was passing away (Gal. 3. 13) together with all that it maintained and presupposed. Another world was coming to birth, the Kingdom was about to begin its existence (Luke 22. 18) and this during the celebration of the Eucharist. This new world was the Church. We shall understand this better if we consider during what kind of meal these events took place.

It was the Paschal supper.[3] The first Pasch had been the signal for the departure of the Hebrew people. They had left Egypt in the name of Yahweh to become the people of God through the Covenant of Sinai. The Twelve at the Last Supper were in a similar position. History was repeating itself and a new Exodus was beginning. It was not Egypt they were to abandon but the mentality of their own race which refused to recognize in Jesus the true Messias and in his community the true Israel and the instrument of God's Reign. They were now to cast aside unbelief and to follow the Son of Man; they were not to look behind them (Luke 9. 62). Further, they were to be moulded into the image of the Son of God (Rom. 8. 29). That is what is meant by becoming God's people, by establishing the Kingdom of God in the footsteps of the Son of David, of Jesus the King.

The Covenant is offered and granted to the Twelve as it was to the Hebrews on Mount Sinai (Exod. 19. 3–8). But

[3] This fact is based on such solid evidence that there is no need to consider the contrary opinion.

it is a new and eternal Covenant. Jesus proclaims it and establishes it (Luke 22. 30) and so fulfils the prophecy of Jeremias (31. 31–4). It is a new Covenant which transcends the former as the Kingdom described by Jesus transcends the Kingdom foreseen by the prophets. The New Covenant like its predecessor is only consecrated and made valid through sacrifice. But it is new, it goes far deeper and it is more complete. There is no longer any question of a mere ritual destruction or immolation (Lev. 16 and 17), but of a return to God through death. The Messias-King will be the first to pass this way (John 13. 1), the Son of God will be the sacrifice, body, blood and soul: "This is my body, which is to be given for you" (Luke 22. 19), "this is my blood, of the new testament, which is to be shed for many, to the remission of sins" (Matt. 26. 28). He takes the lead because he is the King. Thus the Covenant is sealed in blood and the people which follows the Head whom God has chosen becomes, in the blood of the Covenant, the people of God, as on Sinai.

Again as on Sinai (Exod. 24. 9–12), each of the Twelve is now invited to adhere personally to the Covenant and to ratify the sacrifice on his own account by sharing in it in a ritual manner and by spiritually accepting it in anticipation of the day when he will have to give his life back to God as Christ did. And this ritual participation is the communion in the Body and Blood of Jesus Christ. It is for each of the Twelve to become what he receives: "Take . . . and eat", "Take . . . and drink."

This then was how the New Israel was established. Henceforward its destiny is irrevocably fused with our Lord's own personal sacrifice.

The new community is linked for ever to the sacrifice of Jesus Christ, his death and his resurrection. So that no one may be ignorant of the fact, Christ formally declares: "Do this for a commemoration of me." The sacrament of the sacrifice is to be repeated and the efficacy of the Redemption maintained within the Church. It is a duty, and by the same token a power. The eleven who remain—Judas has gone out—are thus given the mission of perpetuating the new Covenant by perpetuating the sacrifice which founded it. This they will do as long as there is a Church, that is, until the end of time (Matt. 28. 20), as long as there are sins to be blotted out, that is, until the end of this sinful world.

All is over. Jesus has said all that needed to be said. What henceforth are the first members of the *Ecclesia*? They are *priests* because they are responsible for the sacrifice and its perpetuation. They are priests in order to bring about the advent of the Kingdom of God through the one sacrifice. They are priests in order to bring to the sacrifice of the Lord that future people whose beginning they themselves are.

But they are also *leaders*. They are leaders because Jesus entrusted to them, and to them alone, the power to celebrate the Eucharist and the duty of assembling the people for the sacrificial celebration. And the duty of governing the Church which is incumbent upon the Apostles had not been overlooked by our Lord. Before the Last Supper the Twelve were expressly appointed as leaders of men, as possessing the power and authority to rule the Church of God (Matt. 16. 18–20; cf. Acts 20. 28) and when necessary to penalize offences (Matt. 18. 15–28).

Priests and leaders, the Twelve are also appointed as *teachers*. By continuing to celebrate the Eucharist in obedience to our Lord's command, they will be proclaiming at the same time that the grace of salvation comes through the Eucharist, they will be teaching also the whole economy of mercy, as our Lord revealed it for the first time when he declared: "This is my Body, which is to be given for you", "This is my Blood which is to be shed for you, for the remission of sins." The celebration of the Eucharist is an object lesson, if we may be allowed the expression, for to celebrate the Eucharist is to declare by acts and by words that salvation is a reality, that the Kingdom of God is at hand, that Jesus Christ is the Saviour, here and now, under the appearances of these rites and in this assembly led by the Apostles or their successors. Moreover, our Lord, long before the Last Supper, had instituted this teaching mission. He had conferred it in terms that are quite explicit: "He who listens to you, listens to me" (Luke 10. 16), and he had repeated it (Matt. 10. 7–27; 18. 18) and applied it to the Twelve as he had done to Peter: "And I will give to thee the keys of the kingdom of heaven; and whatever thou shall bind on earth shall be bound in heaven, and whatever thou shalt loose on earth shall be loosed in heaven" (Matt. 16. 19).[4]

Thus the essential constitution of the Church was completed. Jesus is the lawgiver of God's people. The definitive pattern was laid down, when Jesus had finished the institution of the eucharistic rites and had fully "ordained" men empowered to perpetuate them. Henceforth, as they celebrated the Eucharist—"Do this for a commemoration of me"—the Apostles and their successors would be doing their threefold duty. As the Church's *leaders*, they would have to gather the people of God round the table of the Lord; as *teachers*, they would teach the mystery of salvation by sacramentally accomplishing it; as *priests*, they would continue the work of Redemption in the one sacrifice.

This, then, is the divine law. It is immutable, and in order to preserve it from all corruption, Christ would be

[4] "To bind, to loose", this expression indicates *juridical* and *doctrinal* decisions (cf. *Bible de Jérusalem,* in a note on this passage).

with the Apostles and with the Church until the end of time (Matt. 28. 20).

The supernatural event

We have now followed the visible outlines of the "institution". But the latter of itself has no value whatever. Its transcendent meaning is given to it by the power of God, which transforms Christ's decision into an act that is efficacious for all human history. But this transforming grace had not yet been completely merited by Christ for his Church at the time of the Last Supper. Only his complete sacrifice would be able to secure it, as his own words during the Last Supper suggest.

Hence, when he left the Upper Room, Christ had not yet finished establishing his Church. He had outlined its structure. But the Christian people, present in germ in the Twelve Apostles, was not yet the holy mansion, the people of God, the instrument of salvation. It was in his passion that Christ finally merited this grace and it was in his resurrection that this grace was placed irrevocably at the Church's disposal.

Then and then only was accomplished the "event", then and then only was achieved the absolutely supernatural work of the Church's founding. The coming of the Holy Spirit at Pentecost was to be the final flowering of the Redemption by which the Church was founded.

While waiting for that day to come the Church was still not all that she was intended to be. She could not forgive sins, since the body of the Lord had not yet been "given" for the remission of sins. She could not transmit the gift of eternal life, for Jesus had not yet through his resurrection finally triumphed over death by triumphing over sin. She could not send forth the Holy Spirit because Christ was not yet "the life-giving spirit". ("The spirit had not yet been given to men, because Jesus had not yet been raised to glory", John 7. 39.)

The passion and the resurrection of Jesus Christ were the supernatural "event" which gave the eleven the grace to be a supernatural community endowed with power from God. Henceforth, the source was open from which the first disciples were to receive the strength to remain one, to persevere in the faith and to propagate it, the source too from which they were to receive the impulse and the fervour of charity. And the Apostles were to obtain all these graces not as purely and simply an individual privilege, but as one conferred in their person on the Church as such.

The mystery of Calvary and of Easter is therefore the essential moment in the foundation of the Church. Through it the Church is established in God. In the suffering and risen Christ, she becomes the people of God, the true people which God has willed from all eternity and for whose sake Israel according to the flesh had also been willed by him. The Church becomes the people which renounces the slavery of sin, which preserves faith, hope and charity, she is the "chosen race, the royal priesthood, the consecrated nation, the people God means to have for himself" (1 Peter 2. 9). One with Christ in his passion and resurrection, the Church is to be his Bride forever (Eph. 5. 23–30).

By the same token, the Church becomes the efficacious instrument of salvation. One with Christ, as is the Bride with the Bridegroom and the Body with the Head, she is the prolongation of Christ. Her existence and her words are henceforth the *Verbum Domini,* the Word of the Lord (Acts 9. 2; cf. 6. 7; 12. 24; 19. 20). Her growth and her activity will henceforth be the gradual coming of the Kingdom of God and the outpouring of the divine life (Eph. 2. 20 *et seq.*; 4. 12–13–15; Col. 2. 19).

These truths which are contained in the Scriptures have been expressed in various ways by the doctors of the Church. Pius XII repeated them in the encyclicals *Haurietis aquas* and *Mystici Corporis*. We need only quote one sentence which links "event" and "institution": "The Divine Redeemer began the building of the Mystical Temple of the Church when, in his discourses, he formulated its regulations. He completed it when he was glorified upon the Cross."[5]

Institution and event

It is now possible to understand why the Last Supper was a decisive moment in the process of the founding of the Church. It is related to the two dimensions in the Church's structure, the "institution" and the "event" of grace. In the Last Supper our Lord sums up all the *institutional* acts he performed during his life, the assembling, training and instruction of the Twelve and the conferring upon them of their mission. All this is found in the celebration that took place on Maundy Thursday.

But our Lord then explicitly gave to all these acts a *charismatic* sense. In the Eucharistic act, all the decisions, all the regulations which he had already formulated, are placed in line with the work of Redemption. In the mystery of redemption, Christ's acts of institution receive from him an eternal value and a supernatural efficacy. When Christ gives the command "Do this for a commemoration of me", he links "this", that is the sacrifice of Redemption, to the "doing" of the apostles, that is, to their judicial and visible activity, to their mission.

[5] Encyclical *Mystici Corporis*. The word "glorified" in this passage becomes perfectly clear if we remember that in St John the word indicates both the physical lifting up of Christ on the Cross, his glorious "rising" from the dead and his ascension.

THE SECOND STAGE IN THE FOUNDATION OF THE CHURCH, AFTER THE RESURRECTION

As we have already said, when Jesus announced that the Holy Spirit would be given to the Apostles to help them to fulfil their mission in the Church, he implied that his Church would not be fully established until the Holy Spirit had come. When Jesus rose from the dead, he was glorified and "in respect of the sanctified spirit that was his, marked out miraculously as the Son of God by his resurrection from the dead" (Rom. 1. 4). He became a life-giving spirit (1 Cor. 15. 45) and could send down the Holy Spirit. It was essential that he should send him for only the Spirit could transmit to the young community the good things "that belong to Jesus Christ" (John 16. 14–15). But the Apostles had to wait for the day of the Spirit's coming.

The institution confirmed

Before that day, determined by the Father on his own authority alone, Jesus, between his resurrection and ascension, returned to his apostles. He set to work again, if we may use the expression, on the institution of the Church, he told the eleven once again what their mission was to be, he discussed with them once more the duties which he had laid upon them, he renewed the powers which he had conferred. Once again, he devoted himself to the task of building his Church.

Before he died, our Lord had said to his Father: "Thou has sent me into the world on thy errand, and I have sent them into the world on my errand" (John 17. 18). Now, when he appeared to the ten apostles at Jerusalem (Thomas was absent), he declared: "I came upon an errand from my Father, and now I am sending you out in my turn." He then breathed upon them and said: "Receive the Holy Spirit; when you forgive men's sins, they are forgiven, when you hold them bound, they are held bound" (John 20. 21–3). These few words are, at least in part, a repetition of those which he had used to confer power upon the apostles: "All that you bind on earth shall be bound in heaven, and all that you loose on earth shall be loosed in heaven" (Matt. 18. 18).

In the same way the risen Christ summed up the powers of teaching and of government, which are now definitively conferred on Peter at the Lake of Genesareth. Solemnly and three times running, Jesus commands Peter to feed the flock of Christ: "Feed my lambs . . . Tend my shearlings . . . Feed my sheep" (John 21. 15–18).[6]

Later still, our Lord spoke again of the apostles' teaching office and underlined another very definite aspect of it: "You are to be my witnesses in Jerusalem and throughout Judaea, in Samaria, yes, and to the ends of the earth" (Acts 1. 8; Luke 24. 47–8). This was the very mission which had been entrusted to them when they had been called to be apostles (Matt. 10. 18–20) and which had been renewed shortly before their Master's arrest (John 15. 27).

There is a lesson to be learned from this rewriting of the statutes of his Church by the glorified Christ, the life-giving spirit. As a kind of prelude to the outpouring of the Holy Spirit, he consecrated the organizational elements of his community. In St Matthew's account, our Lord's last act before his ascension was to confirm the duties incumbent on the leaders of his Church. They were to watch over the people of God, "making disciples", they were to sanctify men, "baptizing them in the name of the Father, and of the Son, and of the Holy Ghost", they were to govern and instruct: "teaching them to observe all the

[6] We may note in passing that the threefold repetition is most probably not merely an allusion to the threefold denial of Peter but the solemn conferring of a mission in juridical form and in accordance with contemporary custom. "To feed" means (see John 10) to govern and to teach.

commandments which I have given you" (Matt. 28. 19–20).[7]

What therefore Jesus, as a humbled and persecuted man, had established in his Church was expressly consecrated in the glory of his resurrection by the Lord, the Judge of the living and the dead, and presented to the Paraclete as an instrument of God's plans.

The "event" of grace: the outpouring of the Holy Spirit

The time came for the Holy Spirit to vivify the instrument prepared by Christ. It was the feast of Pentecost. On that day, the Spirit whose coming Christ had merited was poured out upon the Church. From that time forward, the Church, hitherto confined in the silence of the Upper Room, was filled with life and began to move, as Jerusalem was very soon to discover.

This event recalls the creation of the first man. God had first formed his body and then "breathed into it the breath of life" (Gen. 2. 7). Thus Jesus first formed the body of the Church and now he was breathing into it a soul which was the Holy Spirit.

The Holy Spirit was given to the primitive community as such, the gift was made to the leaders of the Church because they were the leaders and that they might be the kind of leaders which they ought to be (Acts 1. 15; 2. 1; 2. 44–7; cf. John 17). With the coming of the Holy Spirit they were granted a communal and public grace, the grace to be the Church and to profess that they were the Church. This was immediately evident. "So, when the noise of this went abroad, the crowd which gathered was in bewilderment" (Acts 2. 6). Peter then took advantage of the occa-

[7] If we are to understand exactly what this passage means, we have to remember that "to make disciples" is not "to have pupils" but "to gather faithful men together under one's authority". The last part of the passage ("to observe all the commandments which I have given you") makes this clear. The parallel passage in Mark emphasizes the teaching function and mission.

sion. The man who had trembled with fear on Good Friday began to speak, he delivered the message of the offer of salvation, of the duty of repeating the Exodus, of membership with the people of God of which they, the Twelve and the hundred and twenty brethren, formed the Head (Acts 2. 38–40).

Many of his hearers answered the call and became members of the true Israel: "So all those who had taken his words to heart were baptized" (Acts 2. 41), and: "These occupied themselves continually with the apostles' teaching, their fellowship in the breaking of bread, and the fixed times of prayer" (*ibid.* 2. 42). The Church had set out on its journey and was alive. The apostles preached, believers were sanctified, charity towards the less fortunate was practised, all goods were held in common (*ibid.* 2. 42; 4. 32–4), assistance was given to widows (*ibid.* 6. 1–6), the first missionaries were sent out (*ibid.* 11. 19–26), grave sins were punished (*ibid.* 5. 1 *et seq.*).

The Holy Spirit was clearly supporting and consecrating the threefold mission conferred by the Lord Jesus before and after his resurrection, the mission of sanctification, instruction and government. The Paraclete revealed himself as in truth the Spirit of the Lord Jesus "deriving from Christ what he makes plain to the apostles" (John 16. 14–15). Thus, by the outpouring of the Paraclete, is completed that "ordination" which Christ had begun to confer upon the Twelve during his public ministry and which he had brought to its decisive moment when he had said: "Do this for a commemoration of me." The Holy Spirit made these humble men into "Churchmen" and gave them the supernatural courage and power to be "Churchmen".

In this respect Pentecost was the last act in the foundation of the Church. It bore witness to the fact that the institution of the Church and the gift of the Holy Spirit were linked with one another according to our Lord's promise, and that the constitution of the Church and the "event" of grace were always to be interdependent. The Spirit was to inspire the Church and the Church was to serve the Spirit. She would understand his plans and implement them as far as human weakness allowed.

St Augustine asks: "Where then did the Church begin?" and he answers: "Where the Holy Spirit came down from heaven and filled the hundred and twenty disciples gathered together in one place."[8] Oriental theology and that of the Greek and Russian Orthodox communities have been traditionally and rightly conscious of the importance of the mystery of Pentecost in relation to the birth of the Church. "On the day when the Holy Spirit came down", writes an Orthodox theologian, "the society of believers became the Church in the proper sense of the term, that is, a supernatural, theandric society, the Body of Christ."

Although the teaching of the Apostolic See has officially insisted more often on the "institution" of the Church during the earthly life of Jesus, nevertheless the Church as a whole is not ignorant of the fact that she was fully established at Pentecost. On that day, said St Thomas Aquinas, the Church was "planted". St Bonaventure used the same expression. Recently Pius XII, when exhorting Christians to pray especially for the missions on the feast of Pentecost, reminded us all that on that day the Church was founded by the breathing of the Spirit. In 1942 he had already emphasized the importance of Pentecost when our Lord "manifested and promulgated his Church by sending the Holy Spirit upon his disciples in a visible manner" (Encyclicals *Fidei donum* and *Mystici Corporis*).

Christ did not bid farewell to his Church once she was

[8] *In ep. Joannis ad Parthos, P.L.* 35, 1991. It should be noted that St Augustine holds that the hundred and twenty disciples received the gift of the Spirit whereas in fact it was only granted to the Twelve gathered in the Upper Room (cf. the note in the Jerusalem Bible on this passage in the Acts).

established. The promise of the risen Christ remained: "And behold I am with you all through the days that are coming, until the consummation of the world" (Matt. 28. 20). Even before his passion Christ had linked his presence and his sacrifice with the *Ecclesia* for all time in the Eucharist. The Spirit came down upon the Church at Pentecost so as to accomplish Christ's promises, for it was in the Spirit alone that Christ could remain present to his faithful and redeem them from sin and death (Eph. 3. 17). In the Spirit alone Christians would receive the witness of the Father to the Son (John 15. 26; 1 Cor. 12. 3); through the Spirit alone the real presence of Jesus Christ in the Eucharist would be made universal.

The ascension therefore was not a farewell ceremony. Pentecost did not set the seal on separation and absence. On the contrary, both feasts together form the official inauguration of the Church joined in the Spirit to the risen Christ.

THE FOUNDING OF THE CHURCH CONTINUED

The work of Jesus for his Church may be considered as limited to the period between the beginning of his public ministry and the feast of Pentecost. But, from one point of view, the founding of the Church goes beyond these few years and extends over the whole Christian era. The mystery of the Church's foundation reaches and includes all generations one after the other. Though the "institution" was strictly localized during the historical life of Jesus, yet the Church's founding is contemporary with every moment of our history. How then is this mystery to be understood? In what sense is Jesus always at work upon the founding of his Church?

The Church in peril at the hands of men

Christ built his Church and gave her life. But we have

168

to remember that she has the whole of history to traverse before time comes to an end, and this among men since she herself is made up of men. A task that has no limits has opened before her. She is to form the people of God from the mass of humanity, to see that it remains the people of God, and finally to increase it so that it ultimately becomes "perfect manhood, that maturity which is proportioned to the completed growth of Christ" (Ephes. 4. 13). All is done, yet all remains to be done. Jesus was well aware of it for a few moments before his arrest he prayed; "that they may all be one; that they too may be one in us, as thou, Father, art in me, and I in thee". Since the model which the unity of the Church must follow is the union of the Persons of the Holy Trinity, according to Jesus' prayer, then the task is of infinite dimensions. We may even say that it is impossible. Humanly speaking, the Church herself is impossible.

In her struggle to survive the Church is opposed by general unbelief and by the unbelief of Christians themselves. We know how hard the Twelve found it to believe. We know that on the morrow of Pentecost the great majority of the Jews in Jerusalem did not submit. In every age the Church is faced with the same danger and it is a danger from within. How then can oneness of faith be possible and how long could it last after Pentecost?

Another peril facing the Church arises from the sins of every sort which her members commit. Only a world in which sin is not triumphant can survive, for it is by the sin of individuals that families, communities and societies are disintegrated. Inevitably sin will cause the Church to perish also unless our Lord remedies the evil and saves his people from ruin.

He alone and no one else can do this. The body of Jesus Christ, and it alone, was "given for the remission of sins", "for the life of the world". The Church will be preserved from the dissolution and death produced by sin but only through the body of Christ in his passion and resurrection. The Church can only be the people of the last days, the people which will not perish, if the sins of the baptized are washed away in the blood of Christ, if the Church's children receive eternal life in the resurrection of Christ, if Christians are constantly converted by the sacrifice of Redemption. Otherwise the *Ecclesia* will crumble to pieces before the end comes.

And this work of conversion is an urgent one that has to be repeated day by day. Sin enters the Church with the sinner and is continually springing up again within her. This was obvious enough in the infant Church. At a very early date we find Ananias and Saphira, covetous and liars (Acts. 5. 1–10). There were the complaints of the Greek-speaking Christians against those who spoke Hebrew (Acts 6. 1), the divisions among the faithful at Corinth (1 Cor. 1. 10–13), the case of incest, again at Corinth (*ibid*. 5. 1–13) and many other sorry examples. Like a ship on her course, the Church can only continue as she has begun. There is no law of inertia in the supernatural order.

Hence the continued existence of the Church is possible only if Christ continues to build his Church, to found it by transforming men's hearts, by converting their souls. In this sense, the founding of the Church cannot be an act that took place purely and simply in the past; it must be ceaselessly begun all over again.

The eucharistic mystery

This is precisely what happens. Christ is at work and every day (John 5. 17). He planted the tree of the Cross in the midst of the Church on the evening of the Last Supper, and he planted it for all time when he said "Do this for a commemoration of me". And now whenever the eucharistic rites are performed, our Lord makes present the sacrifice of

the past and transmits the supernatural power of the passion and resurrection to mankind. In the eucharistic action the work of redemption is continued, is extended indefinitely. It is carried one step further every time "this is done in commemoration of Jesus Christ".

And it is he himself who returns to us—"This is my body"—he who suffered and died under Pontius Pilate, who rose again and is always living to make intercession for us. On the Lord's day, through his apostles and their successors, Christ the Head of the Church invites his people to the assembly of salvation, just as long ago he invited his apostles to the Last Supper. When the faithful are gathered around him, our Lord gives them his Body and his Blood, just as he did to the Twelve—"Take ye and eat"—so that all may become like him as far as human weakness will allow.

This is what is meant by "communion". Christ gathers us all *around* him but also *in* him by faith, hope and charity. Our Lord, who in each of us is one and the same, is the real though invisible bond of our unity. In our Lord and in all those who receive him in communion there is the same Spirit, the same love and the same life. And so the people are made one with their Head, the members of the Body are united both to their Head and to one another. They are cleansed from the hatred that separates and brought together in oneness of soul. This is how the Church is continually being founded, as it was founded on the day of the first Eucharist. "The one bread makes us one body, though we are many in number; the same bread is shared by all" (1 Cor. 10. 17).

It is Christ who builds the Church in the Eucharist, but he does not build it without our assistance. He expects and requires every baptized person to work with him. Each is to be made like to "the image of the Son of God who is our peace", who reconciles us all in one Body by the Cross.

Here the mystery of the Church takes possession of each believer and it surrounds and controls his whole existence.

So Christ continues day by day the work which he began twenty centuries ago. Every day he sends down the Holy Spirit to gather his people together, to preserve it in truth and in charity. If he ceased for one moment to do this, God's people would turn back to its earthly passions, to its disorders and its divisions. Scattered (as it so soon was) over the whole face of the earth, it would no longer be the people of God; the Church would no longer be the Church. To prevent this disaster, Christ is always at work building his Church in the eucharistic mystery.

Our mystery

In the eucharistic mystery the foundation of the Church becomes our mystery and our duty. The building of the Church continues throughout time and presents itself as a task which is always contemporary, as the work proper to each generation of Christians. In the celebration of the Eucharist the founding of the Church is and must be begun again by the men of every age.

This is the vocation of the believer as a member of the Church. He is to share, in sacramental communion, in the redeeming sacrifice and in the founding of the Church. United to the Son of God, the Christian fulfils his personal mission, that is, he becomes a sacrifice as did our Lord Jesus; in him he becomes a force which links him to others, and a glowing fire of charity; like Christ he becomes a light to lighten the faith of others.

CONCLUSION: THE FOUNDING OF THE CHURCH AS A SACRAMENTAL MYSTERY

The dimensions of the mystery of the Church's foundation extend to the whole visible and invisible universe and

include the historical as well as the divine, the juridical and the spiritual orders. It is a sacramental mystery.

By the expression "sacramental mystery" we mean that it is an event which the natural light of reason alone is unable to discern, while at the same time it takes place through realities that are obvious to the senses and in a historical context. It is outwardly expressed in human signs which reveal and make present the power of God.

All that we have so far set out leads to the conclusion that the founding of the Church is a sacramental mystery. It will therefore be sufficient to underline certain characteristics of this mystery.

Christ's sacramental action

During his life on earth, Christ performed certain acts, did certain things which brought together the people of God. He imposed duties and granted corresponding powers.

These, then, are the sensible *signs* which signify the way in which the new Israel is constituted. By instituting them, Christ made salvation, and the form in which it is given, available to all. The written and the spoken word, gestures, decisions, regulations, rites, all describe the grace which is to come, offer it, reveal it, and in this sense are the signs of the salvation which God sends us in Jesus Christ.

But they are not mere signs, empty words and gestures. What Jesus signifies and prescribes, that he effects and he makes real. "My words are spirit and life", our Lord himself said (John 6. 63). The words which Jesus pronounces, the gestures which he makes, derive their efficacy from the passion and resurrection. They become causes of grace in the mysteries of the Son of God. The sensible signs *effect* what they signify. They are sacramental signs.

Thus, when Christ promises infallibility to his Church, she receives it. When he declares that the sacrifice of

Redemption will be made contemporary with every generation, the grace which he proclaims is granted, the work which he announces is done. When he appoints the Twelve as rulers, teachers and priests in his Church, they really become rulers, teachers and priests.

The founding of the Church is not therefore on a par with the drawing up of statutes or with the promulgation of a constitution. It is a sacramental mystery in which the acts of institution effect what they signify, they operate *ex opere operato* and confer the divine grace which they announce, because they are the acts of the Son of God, our Redeemer.

Although Christ himself never administered the sacrament of baptism, we can, without using any paradox, say that he never ceased to administer the sacrament which makes the Church everlasting by "ordaining", sending forth and training the apostles for three whole years. The liturgy of this sacrament lasted during the whole historical life of our Lord and was performed in three stages from the public ministry until the last words spoken at the moment of his ascension. Within the sacrament (that is, the sacrament of the Church) which he was administering, he placed the Eucharist in the front rank. It was a culminating point for which he made long preparations, explaining it with great care (John 6 and Luke 22). The Apostles were the first to receive and benefit by these sacramental rites and on behalf of the generations to come.

The primordial sacrament instituted and administered by Jesus Christ was therefore the fact of the indefectible Church and this was the character which he conferred upon the twelve sons of Israel. Then the whole human race passed over to the New and eternal Covenant. For those who can discern absolute reality, the central thread of human history, past, present and to come, is the building of the Church by Jesus Christ and by those whom he has sent.

CHAPTER III

THE MYSTERY OF THE CHURCH IN CHRIST

We can now come to the central question; what is the nature of the Church?

To many people this question seems to have little significance. If we wish to know what the Church is, they think, all we have to do is to open our eyes and examine the way in which she functions. And we see an international society, organized and possessing a hierarchy, grouping under the direction of a supreme head four hundred million members. The Church has power. Some rejoice at this since it seems to them that the strength of the Church is at the service of the moral order or of a political system of which they approve. Others view it with anxiety and are irritated by it as soon as its power appears to be in opposition to their undertakings.

For all Christians the question is extremely important. Yet not all give the same answer to the question. Protestant thought inclines to the view that there exists a genuine incompatibility between the natural and the supernatural orders, between grace and nature, between the institutional and juridical aspects and the "event" of grace. We are not concerned here with the reasons adduced to justify this attitude. We merely have to consider its effect on the concept of the Church. And it is as follows; the organization of government and of jurisdiction cannot belong to the Church essentially. Nor is it possible that the magisterium exercised by certain members of the hierarchy of jurisdiction should be an intrinsic part of a divine Church. In the Protestant view, we shall be proved right if we adhere to the fact that the Church is a reality in the spiritual and interior order, that it is essentially composed either of the elect and those who will be the elect in the future, or of the just who here and now have made their peace with God. Thus understood, the Church of Christ is withdrawn from the earthly plane and has its authentic existence in the mystery of God who calls his elect to himself. This was the opinion of John Huss before the Reformation in the fifteenth century. Or else she leaves the realm of appearances and exists in the secret places of men's consciences, while in the realm of the visible there are communities which are called "churches" but whose link with Christ is only a loose one. This was the opinion of Luther in the sixteenth century.

In any case, a separation is made between the Church as the "event" of grace, and the churches as human communities. These two orders are not essentially interdependent. No doubt the Church may be called "the Body of Christ" if we are anxious to keep to St Paul's terminology. But this name is used only with certain reservations by Luther. This is understandable since the term "Body of Christ" implies a Church with a visible structure.[1]

In the Greco-Russian Orthodox Church, we sometimes find expressions very similar to those current among Protestant circles. It is a fact that the thought of the Christian East is particularly sensitive to the reality of the divine

[1] We admit that we are giving too summary and too rigid an account of Protestant thought which is at present complex and fluid on this subject.

mystery in the Church, and rightly so. By the same token, many thinkers are less interested in the institutional aspect of the Church.

If we now consider the opinions found among Catholics, it is not difficult to identify the same tendencies, less marked of course, but nonetheless real.

Some people, apparently obsessed with the institutional apparatus of the Church, that is, by her "administration", seem to find it extremely hard to discover anything else in the Church. Others are tempted to introduce a Protestant separatism between the institutional elements of the Church and the mystery of grace. They willingly accept the latter but are ready to look with suspicion on the former, and they claim to go beyond the institutional order in order to come more directly to the charismatic order. They bitterly deplore the existence of a juridical organization, reproaching it, not entirely without reason, for being too slow and too cumbersome. If pressed, they would almost be prepared to hold that all the deficiencies in the Church should be attributed to this cause.

Finally there are others who give way to an excessive mysticism and go so far, in their insistence on the fact that the Church is the Body of Christ, as to identify each individual Christian with Christ.

Such then is the range of opinions and tendencies among those who discuss the nature of the Church. Even though our account of their views is somewhat simplified, it does at least make it possible to realize that the nature of the Church is a matter for discussion. What then is the Church? No doubt all Christians, Catholics, Orthodox and Protestant, admit that she is the Body of Christ. But what are we to understand by this expression?

THE CHURCH, THE BODY OF CHRIST

Before answering this question, we need to preface it with another: Does the Church instituted by Christ know that she is the Body of Christ, does she believe that she must be recognized as the Body of Christ? The answer to this question will save us from following false trails. In fact, the Church's magisterium has on several occasions adopted a definite position and given an affirmative answer. The most recent declaration upon the subject, and the most important, is that of Pius XII in 1943, in the Encyclical *Mystici Corporis.* While the war was still in progress, the Sovereign Pontiff declared that all generations of men were called to unity and peace in the Body of Christ which is the one holy, Catholic, apostolic and Roman Church. Pius XII was not the first to set forth this truth. Others before him had expressed themselves more succinctly, Pius XI in the Encyclical *Mortalium animos* (1928), Leo XIII in *Divinum illud* (1897), and centuries earlier Boniface VIII in the Bull *Unam sanctam* (1302), to quote only the best-known texts.

Although the expression "Body of Christ" has acquired the adjective "mystical" during the course of the centuries, this does not involve any change in the Catholic belief which goes back to the Fathers of the Church who, in their turn, derived it from the teaching of St Paul.

The Apostle of the Gentiles expressly used the term "the Church, the Body of Christ" only in his last epistles, to the Colossians and to the Ephesians (between 60 and 62 A.D.). In these last two letters, he sometimes speaks of Christ as the Head of the Church, which implies that the Church is the Body of Christ, and sometimes he explicitly writes: "the Church, the Body of Christ" (Col. 1. 15–20, 24; 2. 19; Ephes. 1. 18–23; 2. 14–16; 4. 4; 12. 15–16; 5. 21–3, 30).

In the earlier epistles the same idea is most certainly present, but in a more implicit way. St Paul declares: "You are the body of Christ"; he writes: "your bodies are members of Christ". These last two phrases are taken from the

Epistle to the Romans, composed in 57–8, and from 1 Corinthians composed in 57 or shortly before.

Nobody any longer denies that these various ways of expressing the doctrine are the result of a deepening awareness of the meaning of the light which Saul the persecutor had received on the Damascus road. It was then that he learned that Jesus is one with his faithful people.

And is not the statement that the Church is the Body of Christ already implicit in the story of the foundation of the Church as we have retraced it?

It is a fact that, during the years in which Christ was founding the *Ecclesia*, the latter took on her form and consistency in proportion as our Lord's mission was more clearly developed. To be more precise, while Christ was revealing her divine structure and explaining her redemptive function, the Church herself was only at the stage of organization and institution. But when our Lord had reached the glorious goal of his life, when through death he had won for his human nature all the privileges of the Godhead, when after his resurrection Christ had become "a life-giving spirit", then the Church ceased to be dumb and inert; she became alive, she began to spread through the world. Henceforth, her voice was "the Word of the Lord" (Acts 6. 7; 12. 24; 19. 20); henceforth, she was engaged in the work of sanctification (Acts 2. 37–41, etc.).

There is therefore a parallel between the gradual emergence of the Church and the events of which the soul and body of Jesus Christ were the subject. It is as though the Church could not fully be herself until Christ had become "the Son of God, in respect of the sanctified spirit that was his, by his resurrection from the dead" (Rom. 1. 4). In noting this parallel we are led to think that it is based on a close relation between Christ and the Church and that the Church is essentially one with Jesus Christ.

Was this relationship only transitory? Did it only last

from the baptism of Jesus until the ascension? Or was it a definitive relationship? Was the Church one with Christ's humanity for a few years only, or is she still one with it and for ever? These questions are answered by the sources of Revelation and the magisterium replies: the Church is and can never fail to be the Body of Christ. Her very definition is "the Body of Christ".

What then are we to understand by this article of faith? The words do not immediately yield their secret to a Latin mind. And the definition does not at once reveal the real mystery to any human mind. It is well known that among Christians the answers are not unanimous. Yet the Catholic Church has meditated for twenty centuries on these formulae in the light of the Spirit which leads into all truth; and so there are some facts that are certain and an overall view is possible.

THE BACKGROUND OF THE TERM "THE BODY OF CHRIST"

This overall view requires that we do more than consider merely the words "Body of Christ". The context in which they were revealed is equally important. If we are to find their full sense, we must discover the divine intention that is incarnate in them.

Scripture provides sufficient evidence that here as elsewhere God intended to reveal what *he is* for men, namely the Love that saves them. "God is Love." This is the substance of the whole of Revelation. This is also the substance of the message which reveals the doctrine of the Body of Christ. Hence Pius XII summed up the teaching of Revelation on this point when he wrote that the Church is the permanent witness to the divine charity towards mankind (the Encyclical *Haurietis aquas*).

It is this witness which Christ established when he built

his Church as a habitation in which he was to be "the first-born among many brethren". By building his Church, Christ reveals to man the innumerable facets of "the unfathomable riches" (Ephes. 3. 8) of divine love. And charity, like divine wisdom, is infinite in its manifestations.

There is the love which acts and builds, for it desires for God's children a spiritual centre which will be their shelter and their family home. So Jesus stands forward as the architect and builder of the house of God, the house of the people. He makes himself the foundation (Mark 12. 10–11; 1 Cor. 3. 11), so that on and with him in a common task the faithful may build and erect the Body of Christ (Ephes. 2. 22; 4. 12 *et seq.*). The Church, which is the fruit of this love, will be *God's Temple.*

There is sacrificial love. Jesus Christ gives himself for his Church, even unto death and the death of the cross. St Paul understood this perfectly when he wrote: "Christ shewed love to the Church when he gave himself up on its behalf. He would sanctify it" (Ephes. 5. 25–6). Our Lord loved and cherished his Church more than the best of bridegrooms loves and cherishes his bride. The Apostle continues: "A man . . . keeps (his own flesh and blood) fed and warmed." He is referring here to the love of the husband for his wife, and he adds: "and so it is with Christ and his Church" (Ephes. 5. 29). Thus Paul returned to the image which God had used in the Old Testament to express his love for the chosen people. Osee has some admirable words on the subject (Osee 2; cf. Ezech. 16). But now, under the New Covenant and for its sake, charity rises to its highest point which is total sacrifice. "This is the greatest love a man can show, that he should lay down his life for his friends" (John 15. 13). When history comes to its end, Christ will take to himself the Church which he has bought at the price of his own blood. Then she will be fair as a bride adorned for her husband (Apoc. 21. 3 and 9).

The Church, the fruit of sacrificial love, is the *Bride of Christ*.

Finally there is the love of union, the love which transforms and makes men divine. Jesus reveals it in his discourse on the vine. The Jews were very familiar with this image, since they had read of it in the Old Testament where the vine signifies Israel. Like a landowner conscious of the riches he possesses, God watches carefully and sometimes anxiously over this vine. The vine is his treasure and he sets his hopes upon it. Christ returns to the image and perfects it. It now teaches the lesson of transforming union: "I am the vine, you are its branches . . . if a man lives on in me, and I in him, then he will yield abundant fruit . . . It was not you that chose me, it was I that chose you. The task I have appointed you is to go out and bear fruit, and fruit which will endure" (John 15. 5–16 *passim*). The image is enriched still more and deepened by the words that introduce and accompany it: "I will not leave you friendless, I am coming to you" (John 14. 18). In these words we sense the silent beating of our Lord's very human heart so full of love for his own. He adds the following sentences which reveal the mystery of union: "The man who loves me is the man who keeps the commandments he has from me; and he who loves me will win my Father's love, and I too will love him, and will reveal myself to him" (John 14. 21), "and we will both come to him, and make our continual abode with him" (John 14. 23). A few moments later, in the long prayer just before his arrest, Christ returns to this theme of unifying love, which he shows to be the constituent element of the universal Church. And he asks his Father to complete this great work. The Church as the fruit of this transforming love is *the vine* whose life is that of the Son of God himself.

And, to bring this brief meditation to an end, we add that Christ's love is without repentance, it never diminishes:

"I am with you all through the days that are coming, until the consummation of the world." It is the New Covenant and this Covenant is eternal like the charity of God.

It is against this background that the expression "Body of Christ" stands revealed. This must be borne in mind if we are not to reduce the expression to a mere label or an abstract concept.

WHAT DO THE WORDS "BODY OF CHRIST" MEAN?

We still have a long way to go if we are to have a clear idea of the full sense of the expression "Body of Christ". Is it a metaphor or does it indicate something real? If so what is the reality in question?

The thought of St Paul

If we are to answer these questions, we must first of all return to St Paul and ask what he meant by it. We can discover this by examining his thought as it is found in Colossians or in Ephesians, and then comparing it with the earlier uses of the words in Romans and in 1 Corinthians.[2]

What is the "Body of Christ" which the author of these epistles has in mind? It is the assembly of believers gathered together in the same faith in the name of the Lord Jesus. The word "Church" is not applied here merely to the local community at Ephesus, Colossae or Corinth, it is applied to "the Church of God", that is, to the Church universal wherever it may be, the Church of which the Ephesus, Colossae and Corinth communities are cells. It

[2] We refer the reader once and for all to L. Cerfaux, *The Church in the Theology of St Paul,* 1959; L. Malevez, "L'Église Corps du Christ", in *Recherches de Science Religieuse,* 1944; P. Benoît, "Corps, Tête et Plérome dans les épîtres de la captivité", in *Revue Biblique,* 1956; J. A. T. Robinson, *The Body, a Study in Pauline Theology,* 1952.

is this universal Church of which Christ is the Head, as Paul says in the same epistle to the Ephesians. It is this Church which is the Body of Christ, the Church which is found everywhere (cf. 1 Cor. 12. 28), even though it only exists in its local communities (there are differences of opinion on this point among Catholic exegetes, but there is no need to go into the details of this controversy).

There is a further point of importance. In St Paul's thought, is the assembly of the faithful an organized body, an assembly of men inspired by the Spirit, but without any institutional framework? There can be no doubt about the answer. Even among Protestants, the majority would now subscribe to the formula put forward by one of them: "Paul was never 'a brother of the free spirit'" (P. H. Menoud). Moreover it was enough that Paul, like all the Christians of his time, was convinced that the Church took the place of the people of God, for him to avoid imagining that the assembly of the Christians was a riotous horde of people who chanced to be travelling together in the same direction. The Apostle does not gainsay the existence of charismatic gifts at Corinth, he does not deny or disapprove of the fact, but he does not admit that those in possession of the charisms govern the community. Still less have they the right to govern it in opposition to or over the heads of the apostles. This Paul would not have tolerated. The Church is an "order", an organism in which the Lord has appointed some to be apostles, others to be prophets, others to be evangelists, or pastors, or teachers. They are *to order* the lives of the faithful, minister to their needs, build up the frame of Christ's body" (Ephes. 4. 11–14). It goes without saying that harmony and cohesion in this Body are the work of our Lord alone, but this harmony and cohesion are genuine: ". . . the body . . . is unified by each contact with the source which supplies it . . . each limb receiving the active power it needs" (Ephes. 4. 16;

Col. 2. 19). Thus there can be no question of confusing the various "joints" or of usurping their functions. Paul repeats that there is a hierarchy: "Apostles and prophets are the foundation on which you were built, and the chief cornerstone of it is Jesus Christ himself" (Ephes. 2. 20).

This is not the first time that Paul had reminded his readers of the existence of degrees and definite ranks whose order nobody has any right to disturb, for "we, though many in number, form one body in Christ, and each acts as the counterpart to the other" (Rom. 12. 5). These latter words are an invitation to respect the order of functions in the Church. The same invitation is found in the epistle to the Corinthians in which Paul ends his explanations about the organism of the Church, and his pleas for unity, with the following words: "And you are Christ's body, organs of it depending upon each other. God has given us different positions in the Church; apostles first, then prophets, and thirdly teachers" (1 Cor. 12. 27).

There can be no doubt about the conclusion; the social reality which Paul calls at one and the same time "Church" and "Body of Christ", is an articulated institution in which there are leaders and degrees of authority. As for Paul himself, we know that he had no intention of allowing any invasion of the rights which he possessed for his apostolic mission, and it was not unusual for him to exercise them in a very forceful manner.

But we should not have completed our survey of St Paul's point of view if we failed to inquire what further ideas are conveyed by the term "Body of Christ". We have just seen that it is closely connected with the idea of hierarchy, organism and functions.[3] Are there other ideas

[3] Why was the term "Body of Christ" applied by St Paul to the Church? Was he influenced by the classical fable of the "limbs and the stomach"? This problem has caused much ink to flow. It is not impossible that Paul knew the fable. But it is more certain that it was from the point of view of the Eucharist, the Body of Christ, that Paul hit on the expression "the Church, the Body of Christ".

bound up with the term "Body of Christ" or closely linked with it?

A modern reader of St Paul's writings, when he reads that the Church is the Body of Christ, immediately thinks that the term indicates a gathering of men met together for a common purpose, to transact some particular business. He inevitably has in mind a "constituted body" or "a body of troops", etc., and he gives the words "Body of Christ" a similar sense. But the word "body" in St Paul's writings never has the meaning of a group of men forming a "corporate body" united for a common purpose. Still more important is the fact that this sense is unknown to both the Old and the New Testament. There is thus no reason at all for reading this meaning into "Body of Christ" as used by the Apostle.

But what, then, is the immediate sense of the term? The answer is: the most obvious sense. The "Body of Christ" is Christ himself in person, the one Christ who suffered, died, rose again and over whom death has henceforth no dominion. To prevent another misunderstanding, we underline the fact that "Body of Christ" indicates Christ in his humanity, both body and soul, and in his divinity. The word "body" is understood by the Semitic mind as applying to the concrete individual being as a whole.

We have only to draw the inevitable conclusion, however amazing it may seem. Paul asserts that the Church, the assembly of the faithful and a visible organism, whose ministers form a hierarchy, is identical with the Christ of history now risen and in glory.

Are Christ and the Church identical?

The statement that the Church is the Body of Christ is a baffling one, if we take it in its literal sense. Did St Paul mean to tell Christians that there is a genuine identity between Christ and the Church? We shall have gone some way towards the answer if we find we have to admit that Paul's "gospel" as a whole leads us to recognize this identity and that the statement "the Church is the Body of Christ", is not therefore an isolated phenomenon.

A few references will be sufficient. Nobody can possibly doubt that in St Paul's writings we often come across statements such as: to be a Christian is to be buried with Christ, to be one with Christ in his death, in his resurrection, to be included in the mystery of Christ. One passage states this more eloquently than any commentary: "We have to be closely fitted into the pattern of his resurrection, *as we have been into the pattern of his death*" (Rom. 6. 5).

This sentence was written in the context of baptism. It is in baptism that this event takes place (Rom. 6. 1–8), but it also occurs in the Eucharist: "We have a cup that we bless; is not this cup we bless a participation in Christ's blood? Is not the bread we break a participation in Christ's body?" (1 Cor. 10. 16–17).

Paul does not understand this union in a purely moral sense as a mere union of thought and affection, but in a far deeper sense which we must call by the somewhat cumbersome name of "ontological". He wrote: "We have been closely fitted into the pattern of his resurrection", and elsewhere "but if Christ *lives* in you" (Rom. 8. 10), "and yet I am alive; or rather, not I; it is Christ that *lives* in me" (Gal. 2. 20), "no, we are his design; God has created us in Jesus Christ" (Ephes. 2. 10).

To sum up, when St Paul writes of our relations with Christ, he does so in an undeniably realistic way which is very baffling to the modern mind. His realism is compressed into a short formula which is typical of the apostle's mind: "in Christ", "in Christ Jesus". This realism must not be watered down if we are to understand the sense of Paul's thought. Paul uses these realistic formulas in order to make Christians understand that they are an assembly of men which is truly Christ, and that the Church is a living being in which Christ's own life flows.

In other contexts Paul returns to the same thought, but develops it from a historical point of view. The growth of the Church extends through time and Christ himself acquires his full stature in the growth of the Church. Thus there is an evolving Christ, the New Man, or if we prefer, the New Humanity in search of its members (Ephes. 4. 15). From this standpoint, the Church is the human "space" which Christ fills (Ephes. 1. 22).

A famous passage in St Paul sums up and gives the essence of his thought: "The Church", he wrote, "is his body, the completion of him who everywhere and in all things is complete" (Ephes. 1. 23). This passage may be understood in two ways. According to the first, the Church is the "space" filled by Christ. The Church is his fullness because Christ fills her with his presence. According to the second interpretation, the Church is the "space" in which Christ brings about his own fulfilment.[4]

In the first case, the Church is filled and therefore *fulfilled by Christ*; in the second, she *fulfils Christ*. Both interpretations indicate the same Church with its hierarchical organism, its system of functions, its exercise of various powers, its assembly of the faithful. It is this *Ecclesia* which is Christ. She *fulfils* him, because she is of one nature with her Head and continues Christ throughout time; she is *fulfilled by Christ*, because she is one with her Head and is filled with the fullness of Christ.

[4] L. Malevez, "L'Église Corps du Christ", in *Recherches de Science Religieuse,* 1944, p. 65. The first interpretation is more certain from the exegetical point of view. The second has in its favour the fact that the Fathers of the Church accepted it. And this is understandable since it is completely in keeping with the Apostle's thought as a whole in Ephesians, where Paul shows that Christ is in process of fulfilment and that he still has to reach the fullness of his growth.

St Paul throws this truth into astonishing relief. He had not forgotten the lesson which he learnt on the Damascus road, when Christ revealed himself: "I am Jesus whom Saul persecutes" (Acts 9. 5).

HOW IS THIS BROUGHT ABOUT?

Although it is to divine revelation alone that we owe our possession of the truth about the Body of Christ, we are not forbidden to understand the reality as far as this is possible for our human weakness. Thus the Blessed Virgin asked the angel Gabriel who had announced to her the mystery of the Incarnation: "How shall this be?" And we too ask: "How can Christ and the Church be identical in any way?" And our question, like our Lady's, receives the answer: "The Holy Spirit will come. . . ."

And that is the source of every answer in this search. The mystery of the Incarnation, like the mystery of the Church, leads the believer to the Holy Spirit. It is in him that divine things which are impossible to man are easily accomplished. This was the explanation St Augustine gave to the congregations who listened to his sermons.

The Church is the Body of Christ, in the Holy Spirit

Since St Augustine, the doctor of the mystical body, invites us to do so, we shall reflect on the work of the Spirit.

In the Holy Trinity, the Spirit is the bond of love which unites eternally the Father and the Son. The Spirit is the subsistent "mutual love" of the Father and the Son. In him and through him, there is a perfect communication between the Father and the Son, *admirabile commercium*, of which communication between human persons, even when we consider it to be complete, gives us scarcely an idea. The Holy Spirit is the loving unity of God, the giving and the receiving of one another's love by the Father and the Son.

Hence the Holy Spirit is essentially God as communicable, as "givable", if we may so put it. St Cyril of Alexandria attempted to explain these facts by a delightful metaphor: "The Holy Spirit is like the perfume of God's essence, God's living perfume, a living and active perfume which brings the things of God to creatures and himself assures them of a share in the Substance that is above all that is" (*In Joannem*, XI, 2, *P.G.* 74. 452–3. Cf. St Thomas, *Contra Gentiles*, IV, chapter 21). Hence St Thomas also declared that the most expressive word for the Holy Spirit is "The Gift", while Augustine, with the same idea in mind, calls him "Grace", that is gratuitous gift, the divine favour (*Sermo* 144, l. 1, *P.L.* 40. 191). All these terms attempt to show that God communicates himself through the Spirit, becomes present among us and allows us to share in his life through the Spirit.

Since the annunciation, the Paraclete has been the Spirit of the son of Mary, the Man-God (cf. Rom. 8. 9; 2 Cor. 3. 17; Gal. 4. 6, texts referred to in *Mystici Corporis*). He was given to Jesus of Nazareth as he has never been to any other man, and this irrevocably since "Jesus continues for ever" (Heb. 7. 24).

And so the Holy Spirit, who is the Spirit of Jesus, makes Christ communicable, makes it possible for him to be given to us. Through the Paraclete Jesus can become "ours", can be "ourselves" in a certain very genuine sense: "When we are enlightened by the Spirit, it is Christ who enlightens us in him. . . . When we drink of the Spirit, we find we are drinking Christ" (St Athanasius, *First Letter to Serapion*, 19, *P.G.* 26. 573–6). Thus to receive the Spirit is to be moulded into the image of Jesus Christ (Rom. 8. 29), is to live in Jesus Christ, since Jesus Christ himself lives in man with his Spirit and by his Spirit: "It is solely through the Spirit that Christ is formed in us and imprints on us his own features and so makes the beauty of the Godhead come alive again in the nature of man" (St Cyril of Alexandria, *Thesaurus*, 34, *P.G.* 75. 609).

It is in the Spirit that Christians are enlightened concerning Christ, that they recognize and confess that he is the Lord (1 Cor. 12. 3). Thus Christ dwells in the minds who have been converted to his truth (Ephes. 3. 16–17). Again it is in the Spirit that our Lord's desires and intentions are transmitted to the members of the Church and become their desires and intentions. It is in the Spirit that our Lord's own prayer "Abba, Father" (Gal. 4. 6; Rom. 8. 15) continues to be uttered. In the Spirit the faithful contemplate the Son of God and cling to him, for "the Spirit does not show Christ from without, it is in himself that he leads us to know him" (St Basil, *De Spiritu Sancto,* 47, *P.G.* 32. 153). Again it is the Holy Spirit who communicates to the Christian soul the charity whose source is God himself. The love of God has been poured out in our hearts by the Holy Spirit whom we have received (Rom. 5. 5). Through the Spirit, therefore, the charity that comes from God and still is his even when it is given to us (John 17. 26), descends upon us. In the Spirit there is granted to us the love which springs up in Jesus Christ, the love which is his life before it becomes ours and which remains his life even when it becomes ours.

Since the Church has the same attitudes in the Spirit as Christ, since she lives in the Spirit by the same life as Christ, she is the time and space in which Christ continues his existence as the Son of God. "Thus the Body of Christ is the Church. Just as body and head form one individual man, so (Paul) declares that Christ and the Church are one single reality 'in the Spirit' " (St John Chrysostom, *In primam epistolam ad Corinthios,* Hom. 30, No. 1, *P.G.* 61. 250; cf. St Thomas, *In 3 Sentent.* D. 13, qu. 2, art. 1, ad 2). The Fathers of the Church and Catholic theologians express this more briefly by saying that the Holy Spirit is the soul of the Church. This makes it clear that the soul of the Church is not primarily situated at the human, natural, created level, but that it is uncreated, eternal, divine.

In the Holy Spirit Jesus is the Head of the Church

The Holy Spirit communicates Christ to the Church, brings him to the whole world, makes him as universal as the Church, sets him in the context of time to the extent that the Church is in time. Thus, in the Holy Spirit, Christ and the Church are mysteriously and supernaturally one and the same. In the Church Christ is the Head, the Leader, the First. We do not put Christ and the earthly members of his Body on the same level. Jesus Christ is the "First-born", as St Paul says. All the members of the Church, the pope included, are only his humble "brethren". Christ alone is the First and he alone has the right to send the Holy Spirit, since he has acquired this right by his death. He alone can therefore raise the Church to the rank of Bride and make her his Body (Ephes. 5. 25 *et seq.*), because he alone can ask for the Spirit and obtain his request (John 14. 16; 16. 17).

Ever since the Church has been in existence, Christ has not ceased to send upon her the Spirit of God who is his Spirit. In the Paraclete, our Lord actuates, governs, guides and directs his Church.

Christ rules his Church *directly*, inspiring the members of his Body, in the Spirit, to bestir themselves, to consecrate themselves to the service of his glory. Sometimes he prompts them to action which is more adapted to the circumstances of the time, to new methods in keeping with new needs. Christ our Head inspires us all with the same desire: "Father, make thy name known" (John 12. 28). As he sends his Spirit, Christ never ceases to enlighten our faith, to awaken our hope, to give warmth to our charity.

He is "the shepherd, who keeps watch over our souls" (1 Peter 2. 25). The Head's government of the Church here operates through a secret call, an inner inspiration, an invisible actuation spread throughout the whole *Catholica*, the laity as well as the hierarchy (*Mystici Corporis*).

The words "Christ is the Head of the Church" have a further meaning. They declare that, in the Spirit, Jesus rules his Church *indirectly* and *ordinarily* through the successors of Peter and the apostles. The latter have in fact been instituted as visible instruments in Christ's service, so that through them our Lord visibly exercises his rule and gives life, movement and growth to his Body. The government of Jesus Christ therefore is mediated in this way through contingent instruments. And he also becomes incarnate in historical forms. Popes and bishops are only men, yet, through their instrumentality, our Lord directs the whole Body. They are only instruments. They are in no sense equivalent to Christ. This should go without saying. The pope does not "take the place" of Christ, as though the Church had two heads, Christ in the past and the pope today. Such a way of presenting the facts would be absurd and blasphemous. Christ alone can be truly called the Head of the Church (*Mystici Corporis*).

THE PRECISE MOMENT WHEN THE CHURCH BECAME FOR ALL TIME THE BODY OF CHRIST

Where and when did the Church become the Body of Christ? No doubt, an answer to this question has been already given at least by implication. But it should be formulated explicitly as follows. The Church has received from the Son of God her constitution as the Body of Christ in two different ways. Far from being opposed to one another, they are interdependent. The *first* is visible and institutional. It came into being when Christ determined the institutions, mission, powers and duties of the new Israel. The *second* took place in the mystery of our Redemption through Christ's passion and resurrection and the dazzling manifestation of Pentecost.

The juridical mission

In his teaching on the doctrine of the Body of Christ St Paul explicitly proclaims the relationship of the Body of Christ to its institutional aspect as Christ established it. And the sole purpose of this aspect is to provide for the existence and the triumphant vitality of the Body of Christ: "Some *he has appointed to be* apostles, others to be prophets, others to be evangelists, or pastors or teachers. *They are to order the lives of the faithful, minister to their needs, build up the frame of Christ's body* . . ." (Ephes. 4. 11–12).

And this organization is not an adventitious or extraneous element in the Body of Christ, since the precise function of the various ministries and of organization as such is to bring about the growth of this Body. To the words just quoted St Paul adds these which repeat his doctrine in another form: "On him all the body depends; it is organized and unified by each contact with the source that supplies it; and thus, each limb receiving the active power it needs, it achieves its natural growth" (Ephes. 4. 16; cf. Col. 2. 19).

Earlier Paul had pointed out the same relation between the institutional, hierarchical establishment and the living Body of Christ, when he wrote: "Apostles and prophets are the foundation on which you (that is, the Body) were built" (Ephes. 2. 20). Indeed, St Paul had expressed his conviction in this matter, though briefly and implicitly, in the first epistle to the Corinthians (12. 27–8).

In these various passages, he does no more than return to and develop the teaching of Jesus himself. Christ had declared: "Believe me . . . the man who welcomes one whom I send, welcomes me" (John 13. 20). These few words declare that there is an identity between the disciples and our Lord, because they are sent by their Master. On several occasions, Jesus returned to this teaching (Matt. 10. 40; cf. Luke 10. 16). We cannot therefore question the fact that the essence of the Church as the Body of Christ is already implied, proclaimed and realized by virtue of the juridical mission which constitutes her as the Church.

The mystery of redemption

But it is only in the mystery of redemption that the Church becomes completely the Body of Christ in all truth. On the wood of the Cross Christ at a great price earned his title of Head of the Church, by earning the right to give her his Spirit and his life. Then in the glory of his resurrection, he became "lifegiving spirit", and in actual fact gave to her his Spirit and his life. Thenceforward the little band of Apostles was not only a group of friends gathered round Christ, but also the supernatural organism in which flowed the life of our Lord. All those who in the future will be linked to this group with which the Church began will give increase to the Body by their union with its Head. To this whole Body as it grows in size and age, the Head sends the Spirit as he has promised. With the Spirit the Head transmits to all the members "his unfathomable riches", light, love, strength, wisdom. Ever since our redemption was wrought, the life of our Lord has been continually entering into all his faithful.

By his death and resurrection, our Lord joined himself forever to his Church and made her his Body (Ephes. 5. 24). "You are all one person in Jesus Christ" (Gal. 3. 28). Henceforth "You are Christ's body, organs of it depending upon each other" (1 Cor. 12. 27) for the Spirit is in both the Head and his faithful.

Hence also through the redemption, the Church receives

the power to bring to all the world the redemptive power of Christ, just as the body of the Son of Man long ago allowed healing "power to go out of it" (Luke 8. 46). It could not be otherwise, for if the Church has become the Body of Christ, she cannot fail to be an instrument of salvation. Through her, the risen Christ continues to act supernaturally. Through his Body, the Head teaches and redeems.

The Church is what she is by the will of Jesus Christ and she can only continue to be what she is by a permanent act of his will. The Church is the Body of Christ by grace and she remains the Body of Christ by grace. And so day by day Jesus Christ in very fact grants her the grace to be the Body of Christ. And this he does at every celebration of the Eucharist. Christ, who is invisibly present with the congregation and the priest, instils the desire and gives the power to do what he commands. He then comes near to us, offers himself to us in person in communion in order to establish and to strengthen peace and union between the members of the community of the Church. As they receive the one only Lord they receive also the bond of supernatural brotherhood, they become one living body with Christ, in so far, that is, as they allow his Spirit to do his work in them. St John Chrysostom commenting on St Paul (1 Cor. 10. 16–17) wrote in this connection: "We are this very Body [the body of Jesus Christ]. What is this bread? The Body of Christ. And those who receive it, what do they become? The Body of Christ, not several bodies, but one single Body" (*In primam Ep. ad Corinthios,* Hom. 24, No. 2, *P.G.* 61. 200).

CONCLUSION

We have tried to describe this mystery. We must now find a reasonably exact form of words in which to express it. We shall then indicate where, in the concrete, in the time and space which are mankind's context, the Church, the Body of Christ is to be found.

Towards an exact form of words

If we are to discover a suitable (though not exhaustive) formula, we must first dispose of erroneous expressions, and these are of various kinds.

In the Encyclical *Mystici Corporis*, Pius XII protested against an extravagant mysticism which sees in every Christian a personification of Christ. On what authority could such a conception be based? Paul never called an isolated baptized individual "Christ". It is the Church as a whole which is Christ, according to St Paul. It is the universal body "with its joints and ligaments", with all its members, which is called the Body of Christ. Although Paul said: "Christ lives in me", he never said: "I am Christ." This would have been absurd. Jesus Christ's existence as a subject in his own right is never confused with that of individual Christians even when they are acting supernaturally.

Similarly we must put aside all expressions suggestive of pantheism. The Christian, it goes without saying, has no claim to any of the divine attributes. Though it is possible to identify Christ and the Church, this identification is not a natural right, but a free gift, merited solely by the sacrifice of the Son of God. It is entirely a question of mercy and a free gift. And although this gift of grace prevents the Church from ever ceasing to be the Body of Christ, every Christian may break the bond that binds him to the Head of the Church.

There are other misunderstandings which have to be avoided. St Paul's choice of language disallows any crude identification which would lead to a confusion between Christ and the Church. The terms which the Apostle uses clearly indicate the necessary distinction. Thus, the image of the Head implies that it is the Head who commands, governs, rules, while the Body obeys. Or again, the image of the Bridegroom and the Bride shows that the union is not an amalgam or a confusion. Finally, the same is true of the Apostle's statement that the Church is "Christ's *Pleroma*". However these words are interpreted, they imply that the Church is not lost in Christ, since we are told precisely that she completes him and that she is filled by him. The identity between Christ and the Church is not therefore a "physical" identity. To say so would be equivalent to declaring that human personalities cease to exist when they become members of the Body of Christ.

The union of the Church with Christ is essentially *not* a hypostatic union. No doubt the latter is a term of comparison which may help us to have some understanding of the mystery of the Church. But if the formula of the theologian Moehler, "the Church is the Incarnation continued", means that there is a hypostatic union between Christ and the Church, it would have to be absolutely forbidden. In fact the Church is united to God not on the plane of personality, but on that of operation.

Yet in an attempt to avoid these errors, we must not go to the other extreme and reduce the expression "the Church is the Body of Christ" to the status of a mere metaphor, and the solidarity existing between Christ and Christians to a mere "moral" union. The latter by definition would be no more than knowledge of Christ, attachment to his Person, obedience to his commandments. Paul would certainly not recognize his thought in this travesty of it.

What then are we to say if we are to use an accurate formula? Simply this: the union between Christ and the Church is a "mystical" union. This term signifies that the identification between Christ and the Church is a unique reality, that it has no equivalent in the rest of our experience. The union between Head and Body is mysterious, even though we may find some sort of analogy in the union of the members of the human body, and in the union of man and wife in marriage. But Christ's union with the Church is supernatural and for that reason escapes the grasp of our intellect. Hence we have to confine ourselves to the term "mystical", that is supernatural, above nature.

But this does not mean that the union between Christ and the Church is unreal. It is more real than any earthly union, since it is produced by the almighty power of God and is established in that power. It is more real than any earthly union for a further reason; the mystical union is based on God's pledged word and not on man's. Finally it is more real than all earthly unions because it is a participation in the union of the divine Persons with one another. "That they should all be one, as we are one", "that they too may be one in us", our Lord himself had prayed (John 17. 21–3). The supernatural life of Christ's members is not therefore, of itself, on a par with the life of the Head of the Church.

The union is so real, so firmly established that it can never fail. Christ will never cease to be the Head of his Body. On the contrary, his union with it is destined to increase. It is given to the Church not only as a fact but also as a hope. The Body of Christ will "grow up, in everything, into a due proportion with Christ, who is our Head" (Ephes. 4. 15), until it reaches the fullness of its stature when history comes to an end.

Where is the mystical Body of Christ?

If this is so, if the Body of Christ is both a present and a future reality, at what period of time and in what place are we really to find the Body of Christ? In the Last Days and the Beatific Vision? During the course of our earthly history? If so, at what point in that history?

This question only became important from the period

of the Reformation onward. When the Protestants separated the "Body of Christ" and the hierarchical community, the following problem arose: since the Body of Christ is not a given visible and hierarchical community, where is it to be found? The Reformers answered that the Body of Christ is an interior reality, it is justification and a spiritual union with Christ. And so the Body of Christ became invisible.

Who cannot fail to see that this is flagrant disloyalty to St Paul's thought? The Apostle never applies the notion of the Church as the Body of Christ to the justified and the predestined alone, still less to the elect alone. "Body of Christ" is a definition, concise in its wording, wide in its meaning and expressing both the visible and invisible aspects, the functions of the ministry and the supernatural union of the members with one another and with their Head. It refers back to the historical and juridical origin, namely the institution established by Christ and founded on the apostles (cf. John 15. 16).

This is why the Body of Christ can only fully exist in the assembly of the faithful linked to the apostles by the bond of faith, obedience and the sacraments. It cannot genuinely exist where one of these three elements is lacking. Therefore it is only in the one, holy, Catholic, apostolic and Roman Church that the Body of Christ fully and truly exists at the present time.[5] It is this doctrine which is restated by Pius XII in the Encyclical *Mystici Corporis*. It is part of our Catholic faith.[6] "Hence those who believe

[5] In the strict sense, we should say that the Body of Christ is adequately present only in the Catholic Church. This presupposes that the Body of Christ can exist in an inadequate fashion, and at various levels, outside the Catholic Church. This is obviously the case with the Greco-Russian Orthodox body.

[6] Before Pius XII, Pius IX taught the same doctrine in 1861, Clement VIII in 1595. Pius XII returns to it, after *Mystici Corporis* (1943), in the Encyclical *Orientales omnes* (1946), and in the Encyclical *Humani generis* (1951).

they can belong to Christ, the Head of the Church, without a faithful adherence to his Vicar on earth, are in dangerous error" (*Mystici Corporis*). St Augustine had similarly written long ago: "Let them therefore be Christ's Body, if they wish to live by the Spirit of Christ. No one lives by the Spirit of Christ, except the Body of Christ" (*In Johannis evangelium*, tractatus 26, No. 13, *P.L.* 35, 1612).

CHAPTER IV

AUTHORITY IN THE CHURCH

No one who reads the epistles of Paul can fail to be struck by the vitality of the Church, the Body of Christ. To the readers of these letters, the Church reveals her human face, but also her mysterious life, which is the life of the Son of God. We see her physical frame, that is, her ministers and her functions, but also her soul which is the Holy Spirit.

We propose to consider in the Body of Christ those "ligaments and joints" mentioned by St Paul, especially the functions of government and teaching. These two ministries belong to the mystery of the Church, as we have said. They are aspects of it with which we come in touch and they are sometimes exasperating, precisely because of this.

A saying of Jesus Christ raises the problem of our relation to the Church's authority. To those whom he was sending out on their mission, our Lord declared: "He who listens to you, listens to me" (Luke 10. 16). We have met these words more than once and it is time that they revealed their secret to us. Is this sentence merely a figure of speech indicating that the person sent is subordinate to him by whom he is sent, and is the former therefore just an ambassador? Or, on the contrary, are we to take the sentence literally as revealing the identity between the word of him who sends and the word of him who is sent? If the second hypothesis is correct, then Christ meant that his Church is the mediatrix of truth and that she is also the mediatrix of his will for man's salvation. And this brings us once again to the mystery of the Church teaching and commanding.

We must not expect the rational intelligence to welcome the news of an infallible Church. Reason, in fact, finds surprising any pretensions to absolute truth. It considers that a certain kind of scepticism which admits that it has no complete knowledge of anything is more honest. Reason even shows signs of anger and suspects that such a declaration of infallibility is intended to justify some sort of intolerance in the religious and social orders.

Others, who profess Christianity, cannot however admit that Christ's words should be interpreted in a strictly literal way. This is the position of Protestant thought and we must examine it a little more closely.

Luther and Calvin (Luther to a greater extent than Calvin) rejected a hierarchy by divine right, and the existence of a governing authority, as understood by the Catholic Church, continues to be a difficulty for Protestants. Calvin did not deny the infallibility of the Church, but he did deny that Christ had instituted any living organ whose task it was to give authentic expression to his thoughts and intentions. He refused to believe that it is enough to rely on the decisions of a human magisterium, even when it is an ecclesiastical magisterium, so as to discern without error what is revealed truth. According to the Genevan reformer, there is therefore no living and authentic magisterium composed of men. The Councils certainly cannot assume this role, although the earliest of them, in Calvin's view, deserve some credence. The reformer is willing to concede that God uses the Councils, just as he does preachers, to "preserve and maintain the pure preaching of the word".

However if a magisterium on earth has to be recognized, it is not in the hands of men, it is not a living magisterium, it is the Bible. To Holy Scripture must be added the magisterium of the Holy Spirit. The Spirit, acting by way of inspiration, makes it possible for men to discern without error where the true Scripture is to be found and its true sense. The thought of Protestant theologians has not changed appreciably since Calvin's time. If any of them grants that Christ has instituted a living magisterium in the person of the apostles, he adds at once that this magisterium died with them. He thus risks attributing inconsistency to Christ, since, in this view, Christ established a magisterium and then allowed it to disappear at the time when it became all the more necessary.

In any case, in Protestant thought, the infallibility of the Church moves from objective and public expression to the individual faith and the interior life of each Christian. We are therefore inevitably driven to a conclusion to which Calvin would not have subscribed, namely that the Church, the assembly of the faithful, is not infallible in the external profession of her faith. If Calvin would have rejected such a statement, Protestants today commonly accept it. All the churches, in their view, are fallible, no denomination can claim, as a right and as a permanent possession, absolute truth in religious matters. Further, non-Catholic ecumenical meetings seem to be possible only on this basis. Hence when the Greco-Russian Orthodox take part in them, they are something of an embarrassment.

For the Orthodox have preserved intact the primitive doctrine of the Church's infallibility. They add that the infallibility of the Church is manifested in a living and authentic magisterium, that is, in the Councils, but only in the Councils. On this point, they refuse to move and will not admit that any individual, not even the successor of St Peter, has the task of infallibly propounding the truths of faith. In fact, according to the Orthodox there has been no ecumenical Council since the schism between Rome and Byzantium in the eleventh century. It is well known that the Orthodox admit that there is a hierarchy instituted by Christ, and what is more, they have part in it.

The Catholic Church at the Council of the Vatican in 1870, solemnly proclaimed the primacy of jurisdiction and the infallibility of the magisterium exercised by the successor of Peter, the bishop of Rome. There is no need to point out that this is a considerable claim. *A priori* reasons cannot be used to substantiate it. Nor can it be brushed aside merely because it is so extraordinary a statement. In this matter, we have first to acknowledge the will of Christ, to listen to his words and to take note of his decisions. It will then not be out of place to reflect upon this doctrine so that we may obtain a better grasp of our Lord's thought.

THE CHURCH OF CHRIST IS INFALLIBLE

The first truth that we have to confess, and this is a confession common to Catholics, Orthodox and the Protestants of the first generations, is the infallibility of the Church as a whole. It is the whole Church as such which cannot err in regard to faith.

The consciousness of the Church

From the beginning, the Church was conscious that she had been established in final and absolute truth in what concerns the order of salvation. Nevertheless, this Church, as Paul well knew, was not composed of "many wise, in the world's fashion" (1 Cor. 1. 26). Moreover, we know that the disciples of Jesus were manual workers, not men of learning. Yet the author of the Acts of the Apostles did not hesitate, on the day after Pentecost, to call the first community of the faithful "the Word of God", as though that were its proper name, as though this expression provided a definition of its nature (cf. Acts 6. 7; 12. 24; 19. 20). The formula is a curious one and it plainly proves that there existed a conviction which we may amplify as follows: in this small flock and in its faith abides the truth concerning salvation. It can therefore be called, without fear of untruth, the Word of the Lord. So Philip the deacon, to introduce the eunuch to the truth, found that the best thing to do was to introduce him into the Church by baptism (Acts 8. 26–8).

And how could the infant Church have doubted that *her* truth was *the* Truth guaranteed by God himself? She knew that she was the one way of salvation and that it was absolutely essential that men should join her; she professed that she was for all men the only means "to save themselves from this false-minded generation" (Acts 2. 40). If the Church has been made by God the one way of salvation, she is inevitably the way of truth. It is because she is conscious that she is the "way" that she is directly conscious of her infallibility.

In writing to Timothy, St Paul says of the Church that she is "the pillar and foundation upon which the truth rests" (1 Tim. 3. 15). The Apostle was surely doing no more than translating into his own terms the words of our Lord in regard to his Church: "The gates of hell shall not prevail against it" (Matt. 16. 18).[1]

The Church cannot fail in faith, she cannot be deceived by error. As long as the world lasts, the Church will not take any human invention or any purely intellectual theory

[1] The expression "gates of hell (or Hades)" refers directly to the powers of evil. Lying and error appertain to the powers of evil. This is why we are entitled to see in this passage an assertion of the Church's infallibility.

as an object of faith. She will never abandon any single one of the truths revealed by our Lord. This conviction is reflected and expressed by the Vatican Council in the text which proclaims the infallibility of the Sovereign Pontiff. It is stated there that the pope possesses the infallibility "with which the Divine Redeemer willed that his Church should be endowed".[2]

In what precise sense are we to understand the infallibility of the Church? In the sense that the Church, the universal assembly of the faithful, cannot be mistaken in what she believes and professes. It is a *passive* as opposed to an *active* infallibility. When we speak of *passive* infallibility, we are considering the whole Church including the pope and the bishops, since he and they are Christians before being leaders. It is this Catholic community which cannot be mistaken, which cannot take as an object of faith something which in fact is not. When we say this, we are not forgetting that the faith of each individual baptized person may fail, may be mistaken, may take as an object of faith something which in fact is not, or may misunderstand one or other of the truths of faith. We are declaring that the Church as a whole cannot err in matters of faith, either by adding to or subtracting from revealed truths.

The source of infallibility in the Church

Surely these explanations are paradoxical. How, it will be said, can we conceive of a society in which each is able to be mistaken individually, but which is collectively infallible?

Let us say straightaway that it is certain that the Church's infallibility cannot find its explanation in man. It does not rest on the knowledge and intelligence of the faithful, nor

[2] Vatican Council, session IV, chapter 4, Denz. 1839. Previous references: Gregory XVI in 1834, cf. Denz. 1617; Pius VI in 1794, cf. Denz. 1501; Simplicius in 476, cf. Denz. 476.

does it depend on the holiness of the Church's members. Nor is infallibility assured purely and simply by the Church's hierarchical constitution, as though the secret of resistance to heresies and errors were to be found in discipline alone.

The Church's infallibility is a gift of God. "The true light", which is the truth of God in Jesus Christ, has been granted to the Church and confers infallibility upon her. True faith cannot fail the Church nor can the Church fail the true faith because the Church is the Body of Christ and her Head is light and truth. In matters of faith therefore, the Church will be given true discernment and knowledge.

In the Holy Spirit, the soul of the Church, it is the vision of his Father which Jesus possesses, the vision of himself, of the Church, that becomes in some sort the mind of the Church, the Body of Christ. This, then, is the faith, "the hearing of the Word" in the assembly of the faithful. Hence it is completely unthinkable that the whole Church should allow herself "to be like storm-tossed sailors, driven before the wind of each new doctrine that human subtlety, human skill in fabricating lies, may propound" (Ephes. 4. 14). Christ's thought is continued in the Church's thought. If the thought of the whole Church could miscarry, the Holy Spirit would have deceived us when he inspired Paul to write: "You are one body, with a single *Spirit* (*of truth*), . . . with the same Lord, the same faith", and "through faith in *the Son of God, and fuller knowledge* . . . we shall reach *perfect* manhood, that maturity which is proportioned to the completed growth of Christ" (Ephes. 4. 13).

The same thought recurs in other forms and is stated with greater precision. The Church, says Paul, is founded on Christ (1 Cor. 3. 11), who is her corner-stone (Ephes. 2. 20). This being so, there is no reason to fear that error may introduce itself officially into the house of God. Christ has been given to us "to be all our wisdom" (1 Cor. 1. 30), and, today as yesterday, his are the words of eternal life (John 6. 69).

Christ himself provided the essential and permanent guarantee of truth in the Church when he said: "And behold I am with you all through the days that are coming, until the consummation of the world" (Matt. 28. 20). Infallibility is not a peculiar characteristic of the members of the Church, a kind of hereditary quality in which the sons of the Church might find grounds for a certain pride. Infallibility is rather a created phenomenon kept in being by our Lord, a gift freely granted at every moment of the Church's life. It is not a thing, it is an event in the realm of grace like Pentecost, but a Pentecost continued and without external manifestations. Christ has to send his Spirit continually so that true light may be really granted to the Church.

"As long as I am in the world, I am the world's light" said Christ (John 9. 5). And Jesus is in the Church day by day to bring light to the world. He is there in his Real Presence and by his redeeming sacrifice. It is there that he radiates his light and gives his Life to men. For the light comes from the cross and shines in the resurrection.

Christ declared in a general and somewhat enigmatic way to the unbelieving Jews: "When you have lifted up the Son of Man, you will recognize that it is myself you look for" (John 8. 28). We might render this sentence as follows: "When you have lifted up the Son of Man on the wood of the cross (and this lifting up is the prelude and promise of his glorious ascension to the right hand of the Father), then you will be given the full light to enable you to see who I am, to see my divinity, then you will come to ultimate truth". The infallibility of faith, today as in the past, can only come from the passion and the resurrection.

The baptized, plunged as they are into these mysteries (Rom. 6. 1 *et seq.*), are enlightened, *φωτισόμενοι*, as the Greek Fathers used to say. If this is the case in baptism, the infallible light of faith is surely bound to come still more essentially from the Eucharist which is the sacrament of the redeeming sacrifice. The eucharistic mystery is truly *ad eruditionem* (to use the phrase applied in the Middle Ages to all the sacraments); it brings light to our faith. The Eucharist is the supreme sacrament of eternal Life (John 6. 51–8), and eternal life is precisely "knowing thee, who art the only true God, and Jesus Christ, whom thou hast sent" (John 17. 3). If the impossible happened and the eucharistic sacrifice were to cease for ever in the Church, then Christ would cease to send his Spirit to the Church, and the faith of Christendom would gradually disintegrate until it completely disappeared.

The source of infallibility in the Church is therefore sacramental. St Cyril of Alexandria wrote: "Whoever shares in Christ by receiving his holy flesh and his blood will also possess his spirit", which is the Spirit of truth. These words apply equally well to the Church as a whole. They also declare that the foundation of infallibility is sacramental and, more especially, eucharistic.

AUTHORITY AND THE MAGISTERIUM IN THE CHURCH

The faith of Christ's Body is infallible. And faith, according to the thought of the New Testament, is not only an inner and invisible acceptance, it is also and indissolubly an external profession of faith (Rom. 10. 9). Faith is by definition a proclamation. Thus when we assert that the Church's faith is infallible, we are directly asserting that it is infallible in the external confession which expresses in the full light of day and cries upon the housetops the message of revelation.

This is how Christ intended it to be, or at least this is what he implied by his declarations on the unity of the Church. He willed that the unity of faith and charity in his people should be, in the eyes of future generations, the witness to his divine mission (John 17. 21–3; cf. 15. 7, 15; 16. 13). Can we imagine that the unity of faith would express itself in false declarations and yet be at the same time a sign of Christ's own trustworthiness and of his divine mission? This would be absurd. We must therefore acknowledge that the collective faith, collectively expressed by the Church, does express itself infallibly; it will be a confession free from error. This is certainly our Lord's own will.

How then can we avoid the question: where are we to find the authentic and infallible expression of the faith confessed by the Church? Is this expression, free as it is from error, to be found in the word of each individual Christian? But this is impossible, since every Christian may be deceived, may be ignorant of certain articles of the faith, may become a heretic or even completely lose the faith. Is it to be found in Scripture? Doubtless it is, but Christ is not talking of Scripture in the passage to which we have referred. In any case, the New Testament was not yet written when Christ made this declaration. What he had expressly in mind was the witness borne by living men. We have only to examine all our Lord's words to see that he nowhere asked his Church to have recourse to a written document as the sole criterion of the authentic expression of our faith. The apostles for their part, writing at the dictation of the Holy Spirit, never mentioned any such method.

Is the authentic and infallible expression of the faith to be found in the believing Church taken as a whole? It obviously is, as we have shown above. Yet this answer still has an element of obscurity, for the following question is not an absurd one: "Among the divergent voices to be heard in the Church, which are those that authentically express the message revealed through Jesus Christ?" This question was already asked in apostolic times (1 John 3; 2 John 7–11).

The final answer to this question is found in the New Testament and in the history of the Church whose beginnings are described in the New Testament. We see in it how the apostles and their successors understood the structure of the Church, and how their concept of it is justified. We must therefore turn to the Gospels, the Epistles and the Acts of the Apostles.

The infallibility and the authority of the bishops as a body, and of the Sovereign Pontiff

193

In the earliest days of the *Ecclesia* Paul appointed to take his place in certain areas persons invested with authority, Timothy and Titus. They are the apostles' first successors. We may call them "bishops", using our own terminology, although in fact the name "bishop" was not yet given to them. These leaders of the Church in certain regions played a constant and determining rôle in the life of the universal Church. They taught the faithful in their respective districts and they met in provincial or general assemblies (ecumenical Councils), under the presidency of the bishop of Rome or his legates. They were the leaders of the Church, the bishops as we now call them, who, with the bishop of Rome, dealt with questions about the faith. They possessed the right and the duty to speak with authority on these matters and to settle disputes. The leaders of the Church were also, like the apostles, the Church's teachers, her doctors.

From the beginning, the Christian conscience held the Councils and their decisions in great honour. In 1863 Pius IX declared, in a formula that has become classical, the rôle and the authority of the bishops as a body. The infallibility of the Church, he said, is exercised in matters of faith by the extraordinary magisterium, that is, by the solemn definitions of ecumenical Councils and the Sovereign Pontiffs, but also by the ordinary magisterium of the Church as a whole, that is, through the teaching of the bishops scattered throughout the world in communion with the pope. In 1870, the Vatican Council authorized a similar statement and added to it a declaration about the authority of the bishops, the successors of the apostles. During the Modernist crisis at the beginning of the twentieth century, the Holy See again asserted "the most certain existence of a charism of truth which is, has been and always will be, found in the episcopal body that has come down to us from the apostles".

This then, in very summary form, is the Church's thought on the authority to govern and to teach residing in the body of the bishops as a whole.

The part played in the Church by the Sovereign Pontiff was explained at considerable length by the Vatican Council. Thus the already existing faith of the Church in this respect saw itself solemnly sanctioned. After defining the primacy of jurisdiction of Peter's successors over the whole Church, after ruling out the restrictions which past centuries had attempted to place upon it, the Council ended by defining the infallibility of the pope in matters of faith and morals.

We asked where the authentic and infallible expression of the Christian faith was to be found and we now have the answer. The words uttered by the successors of the apostles are the authentic and infallible expression of the Christian faith, when the latter in the exercise of their function as pastors and teachers teach what Christ has entrusted to them. The Church therefore recognizes that Christ has established a living, authentic magisterium assisted by the Holy Spirit in order that it may perform its mission without falling into error. Further, the Church has believed and still believes that the magisterium has been placed in the hands of the leaders of the Church, the successors of the apostles and the successors of Peter. In a word, the ecclesiastical hierarchy is a hierarchy of leaders whose function is also to teach.

The sources of this doctrine

Faith in the authority and the magisterium of the hierarchical Church was first lived and exercised under the guidance of the Holy Spirit before it was expressed in theoretical form. And the faith as lived and exercised was awakened by certain facts and words dating from the origins of the Church herself.

One of the very first of these events is reported in the Acts of the Apostles, and it is the first case of the exercise of her magisterium by the Church. It was, in fact, the first Council, and it took place at Jerusalem in about 48–9 A.D. The assembly had to discuss what should be done about converts from paganism. Should they be obliged to observe the Jewish Law or not? After the deliberations were over, the assembly sent to Antioch a letter which contains the following words: "*It is the Holy Spirit's pleasure and ours* that no burden should be laid upon you beyond these, which cannot be avoided; you are to abstain from what is sacrificed to idols, from blood-meat and meat which has been strangled, and from fornication" (Acts 15. 28–9). In this passage, Scripture is describing the exercise of the magisterium as an institution. The magisterium declares the truth and its decisions are authoritative. It is assured of the assistance of the Holy Spirit and is aware of the fact. It cannot err when it officially teaches, and it derives its assurance from this faith.

Nobody at Jerusalem seems to have been surprised by

this declaration, astounding though it is: "It is the Holy Spirit's pleasure and ours . . . ". Nobody considered this an untenable claim. And rightly so, for had not Christ entrusted to his apostles collectively both authority and the magisterium when he had told them "all that you bind on earth shall be bound in heaven, and all that you loose on earth shall be loosed in heaven" (Matt. 18. 18)? Peter, especially, had seen these same powers entrusted to him personally on an earlier occasion (Matt. 16. 18 *et seq.*). Finally before leaving his apostles at the moment of his ascension, Christ had told the Eleven once again what duties were incumbent upon them; they were to teach, to make disciples, to see that his commandments were observed (Matt. 28. 19–20).

Here then are the sources of magisterial and jurisdictional power. Although some Protestants are less inclined than formerly to dispute this, yet they immediately add that this authority was entrusted to the Apostles alone and that this power died with them.

This is a mistaken view. Christ willed that there should be successors to the apostles in the duties which he was entrusting to them. We agree that he nowhere directly propounded the idea of the "apostolic succession", but he spoke clearly enough to prevent any misunderstanding in the matter.

The Son of Man gathered his apostles together and founded the Church only in order to hand on to them his own mission, that is, his mission to call all sinners to salvation at all times and in all places, since there will certainly be sinners at all times and in all places until history comes to an end. Christ's public and official mission is to bring about the Kingdom of God. When he delegates it, this is not for a short time only, but, like his redeeming mission, for all time. The powers entrusted to the apostles are a share in this mission.

Hence, when he entrusts his mission to the Twelve, Christ does not confer on them a purely personal dignity, but he organizes them in the service of the Kingdom of God, he establishes the functions which are to bring about the fulfilment of the Kingdom. And if this mission is to last for all time, so also will the "services" attached to the mission. This is why the institution of "perpetual services" implies that the apostles are to have successors in their "functions" or "ministries".

Can we imagine Christ conferring anything other than duties and responsibilities in his Church? Can we imagine him distributing dignities and privileges? Where in the Gospel should we find justification for such a wild fancy? Christ gives us "duties", a mission, so that Redemption may come to the whole world. And these duties are services and their names are "magisterium" and "jurisdiction".

These men then will teach and govern and this they will do only with the assistance of the Paraclete. Christ does not establish in his Church secular powers but a holy mission. To those who exercise it, he said: "the Holy Spirit . . . will . . . recall to your minds everything I have said to you" (John 14. 26). It is in the Spirit that the apostles will deepen their faith and allow themselves "to be guided into all truth" (John 16. 13). It is in him that they will continue the work of Christ; "And he will bring honour to me, because it is from me that he will derive what he makes plain to you" (John 16. 14, cf. 15. 15, 27).

It is plain that Christ entrusted both magisterium and government to the same men. The leaders were also to be teachers. The magisterium is not entrusted to men of learning, to specialists nor even to theologians. It is the responsibility of those who govern. Under these conditions, the highest function of the magisterium will surely be bestowed by Christ upon the man who possesses the highest authority in the Church. And this in fact is what Christ decided to do. Peter received both the supreme power to govern and the supreme power to teach. Peter will be the voice of the Church, her official and definitive voice. We cannot possess Christ's truth unless we are at one with Peter and his successors. Christ spoke specifically on this point: "thou art Peter, and it is upon this rock that I will build my church; and the gates of hell shall not prevail against it; and I will give to thee the keys of the kingdom of heaven; and whatever thou shalt bind on earth shall be bound in heaven, and whatever thou shalt loose on earth shall be loosed in heaven" (Matt. 16. 18–19).

This was not the first time when Peter found himself invested with the primacy among the apostles. On more than one occasion he had been named before the others and distinguished from them. The fact is too well known for us to insist upon. But this was the first time when Peter was definitively appointed as the leader of them all and as the guarantor of the entire work which was to be done. In this passage Peter alone receives the task of being the Church's foundation. On him first of all is conferred the doctrinal and disciplinary authority in the formula "to bind and to loose". The other apostles will only receive it after him and in union with one another and with Peter (Matt. 18. 18).

Finally, after the resurrection, when our Lord repeated his instructions about the functions of the apostles, Peter, and he alone, was given the task of feeding "the lambs and the sheep" of Jesus Christ (John 21. 15–18). Peter therefore was definitively endowed with supreme authority in the Church. At the same time and in the same words, he was given responsibility for the exercise of the magisterium (cf. John 10. 3, 15–16).

Peter therefore holds the first place in the Church. He is the leader in a higher sense than the others. Hence the duty of giving expression to the universal Church's infallibility in matters of faith is fully his by right. It is easy to see that Peter's faith is of decisive importance for the Church's life. Christ expressly pointed out how important he intended it to be. He therefore prayed that the apostle's faith should not fail and gave him the task of confirming the faith of all the rest: "Simon, Simon, behold, Satan has claimed power over you all, so that he can sift you like wheat; but I have prayed for thee, that thy faith may not fail; when, after a while, thou hast come back to me, it is for thee to be the support of thy brethren" (Luke 22. 31–2). If our Lord prayed that Peter's faith should not fail, his prayer cannot have remained unheard and unanswered on behalf of Peter and those who were to be his successors.

Thus, when the Vatican Council declared that the Sovereign Pontiff is infallible when he speaks "by virtue of his supreme apostolic authority" as doctor and pastor of the universal Church and defines a doctrine of faith and morals, it was not distorting the original meaning of our Lord's words. Nor when the same Council declared that the whole body of the bishops as successors of the apostles, in union with the Sovereign Pontiff, teaches infallibly, did it pervert the authentic sense of the words of Jesus. Peter's word is the sign by which the Church's faith is recognized, because Peter is the Church's leader. Peter's doctrine is the criterion in matters of faith because the voice of Christ speaks in the word of Peter and the apostles.

Therefore Peter's word or the pope's is not more infallible than the voice of the episcopal body in communion with the pope. Conversely, the body of the bishops in communion with the pope is not more infallible than the voice of the pope alone. The infallibility of the pope and the bishops is not a different infallibility from that of the universal Church taken as a whole. But the infallibility proper to the Body of Christ finds its official expression only in the voice of its leaders precisely because it is the voice of its leaders. This in fact is what the Vatican Council points out in defining the infallibility of the Sovereign Pontiff. It observes on the one hand that the pope exercises the infallibility with which Christ willed that his Church as a whole should be endowed, and on the other hand it notes that the right to provide the infallible Church with a voice is the pope's by virtue of his *supreme apostolic authority*.

This then is what the Church is, and this is where authority is situated in the Body of Christ.

Authority in the Church a sign of Christ's presence

It is doubtless surprising that Christ considered the teaching office should be entrusted to leaders of men. Why did he not call on professionals to teach his doctrine? Governing and teaching are functions which have little in common, and we know of hardly any chiefs of State who were thinkers like Marcus Aurelius.

To those who express astonishment, one may reply that Jesus Christ did not come to found a school and to propagate a theory; Christ was not a professor and the apostles were not students. He was the founder of a people; his aim was to draw the whole of mankind towards its own supernatural destiny. Thus the knowledge which Christ requires of us is not notional and theoretical, it is a spiritual movement, it is knowledge, love and action combined.

An answer couched in these terms is a true one, but it is incomplete since it does not provide a positive explanation of the meaning of authority in the Church. We shall therefore try to make the scope and meaning of authority clear by returning to its source, that is, to what Jesus Christ himself intended it to be.

The people founded by the Son of God is not like any other kind of religious society, Christ's undertaking has nothing in common with those of Buddha and Mohammed. The Messias establishes the people of the Kingdom of God.

Still more, it is *his* Church which he builds, and she is his by an absolute union since she is *his* Body. Christ then is her one Leader because he alone is her Head. He will be her Head until the end of time because he will always remain the corner-stone of the building (1 Cor. 3. 11; Ephes. 2. 20; Acts 4. 11). He is the Leader who commands, the Doctor who teaches, the Saviour who sanctifies.

But, since the ascension, the Head of the Church is hidden in God and invisible to us; the order instituted by Christ is a sacramental one in which divine power is present and active only in so far as it is visibly signified to men. Hence the Head's lordship over the Body must be represented and shown in order that it may be really exercised over the whole Church. Only thus will the members of the Body receive life from the Head. This is the precise function of authority in the Church. It is intended to signify and make present the sovereignty of Christ as Leader, Doctor, Sanctifier.

The Church's responsibilities and her hierarchy are functions which are signs of Christ. This is why the essential degrees of the hierarchy necessarily involve the three powers of order, teaching and jurisdiction. The episcopal body is the image of Jesus as Head, just as Jesus is the image of God.

There can be no doubt that Paul knew this since he wrote the sentence "it is Christ who speaks through me" (2 Cor. 13. 3). He considered these few words too evident to need justification or explanation. For him, the doctors and leaders of the Church continue Christ, they signify the Head and mediate his action. St Augustine also expressed the profound meaning of the pastoral function and the reason for its existence and authority when he declared that the pastors of the Church are only so in and through the one Pastor.

From this standpoint, the meaning of the pontifical

primacy becomes immediately evident. The primacy is not merely a supreme authority owing its existence to the fact that experience has shown the need for a "supreme court". The primacy is to be the sign of Jesus Christ, Head of the Church. This is the sense contained in the text of Scripture, which proclaims that Christ is the Church's one foundation, the corner-stone on which the whole edifice depends (1 Cor. 3. 11; Ephes. 2. 20; 1 Peter 2. 4). Yet Peter also is the Church's foundation, the rock which guarantees its permanence (Matt. 16. 18). It is abundantly clear that Peter cannot take the place of Jesus Christ. He must therefore be the sign and instrument of Jesus Christ, Ruler, Doctor, Sanctifier.

Catholic thought has understood this quite spontaneously. It calls the pope "the Vicar of Christ". This same Christian sense very quickly realized that the function of superiors is to prolong, to make available and to apply the only authority existing in the Church, that of the Son of God. Hence the Christian sees his superiors as "the representatives of Christ" at different levels, of course, according to the circumstances and responsibilities involved.

It follows that authority in the Church is always subordinate to the Church's mission which is to sanctify the people of God, to preserve it as the Body of Christ, to be the "guardian of our souls", like Christ himself (1 Peter 2. 25). In this respect, jurisdiction and magisterium are in the service of the power of order.

THE EXERCISE OF AUTHORITY IN THE CHURCH

To consider the exercise of authority in the Church is not to cease to contemplate her mystery, it is to examine the ways in which the mystery of the Church enters into everyday life through the particular operations of her magisterium and her jurisdiction.

The hierarchy operates in various ways. Sometimes its authority is exercised in pronouncements on matters with which the magisterium is *directly* concerned, truths, that is, which involve faith and morals and are contained in the deposit of Revelation. These truths form the doctrine of salvation and are the *proper* domain of the magisterium. At other times, authority intervenes in matters which are intimately connected with dogma without being formally vouched for by the deposit of Revelation. These truths are the *secondary* and *indirect* subject of the magisterium.[3] Finally, at other times, the authority of the Church intervenes in *temporal questions*. Thus, for instance, it gives a judgement on the desire of colonial peoples for independence. In the latter case we would point out that there is an exercise of the magisterium in so far as a doctrinal judgement is involved, and at the same time, there is an exercise of *jurisdiction* in so far as the practical directives must be followed.[4]

The magisterium

Before examining the concrete conditions in which the magisterium is exercised, we must point out that not every word uttered by the pope is an exercise of the infallible magisterium, even when he is speaking officially. This is all the more true in the case of a bishop since no bishop has the power to put forward by himself and infallibly the truths of faith. Only the whole episcopal body in communion with the Sovereign Pontiff has received the right to

[3] The standard instance of this is found in the five propositions taken from Jansenius' book. The Church defines that they are in fact to be found in Jansenius' book as far as their substance and sense is concerned. (We are only providing a summary account of the operation of the magisterium. Certain aspects of it are debated among theologians.)

[4] The jurisdiction in question is then *indirect*. The term "indirect jurisdiction" has led and still leads to misunderstanding. We retain it here for lack of a better and equally brief expression.

declare authentically and infallibly what truths must be believed.

We now proceed to examine the two ways in which the infallible teaching of the Church is given, namely, the extraordinary and the ordinary magisterium.

The extraordinary magisterium

The form of the magisterium with which Christians are most familiar is the extraordinary magisterium, precisely because it is exercised with great solemnity, either by the pope alone or by the bishops in communion with the pope and gathered around him or his legates.

The extraordinary magisterium is exercised by the pope alone when the bishop of Rome, speaking *ex cathedra* as doctor and pastor of all Christians, proclaims the truths in matters of faith and morals which are to be believed because revealed by God. No mistake is therefore possible, since the pope is under the authority of the Word of God in Jesus Christ. He puts forward nothing that is not contained in the deposit of public revelation and this deposit was closed at the death of the apostles. The task of the magisterium is therefore in general not to "reveal" something hitherto unknown to the Church, but to "propose" to our faith what has been revealed by God. Thus, in the exact sense of the term, dogmas are not identical with "The Word of God", they are the authentic interpretation in human language of the Word of God contained in the revealed deposit.

We must not therefore imagine that revelation is continued through the pope. The Sovereign Pontiff is certainly assisted by the Holy Spirit when he proposes truths of faith, but the assistance of the Holy Spirit does not in any way constitute a continuous revelation, it is only a guarantee against error and the help given to distinguish those truths to which it is necessary to draw the Church's attention. Whatever he does in this sphere, the Sovereign Pontiff does by virtue of his authority, and the approval of the faithful or of the episcopate is not a condition required for the validity of his teaching.

The pope obviously speaks *ex cathedra* when he announces his intention of speaking as head of the universal Church. Yet no particular formula is required to make this clear and there is no kind of protocol in this matter. All that is necessary is that the intention of the Sovereign Pontiff to bind the whole Church should be sufficiently clear. This was the case when Pius IX proclaimed the Immaculate Conception of the Blessed Virgin in 1854 and when Pius XII in 1950 defined her Assumption.

The extraordinary magisterium is exercised by the bishops in union with the pope at ecumenical Councils. The latter are constituted *de jure* when there is a meeting of all the cardinals and all the diocesan bishops. It is not necessary for them all to be physically present for the Council to be valid. But what is indispensable if a Council is to be legitimate and its teaching valid is union with the pope and evidence of this provided by the physical presence of the Sovereign Pontiff or by that of his representatives. Councils exercise the extraordinary magisterium when they solemnly "propose" truths which are to be believed in matters of faith or morals and when their intention of binding the whole Church is sufficiently evident. The Vatican Council exercised the magisterium in this way when it defined the Sovereign Pontiff's primacy of jurisdiction and his infallibility.

The ordinary magisterium

The ordinary magisterium, on the other hand, differs from the extraordinary in that it is not confined to such determined periods of time and to a few documents, as are ecumenical Councils and *ex cathedra* definitions. The ordinary magisterium is exercised continually in the Church. From the beginning popes and bishops have had to teach the faithful committed to their care. In many and various ways, in sermons, books, exhortations and letters, they have proposed, and continue to propose, truths to be believed. Sometimes their doctrinal teaching appears in a condemnation, sometimes in the form of a declaration of adhesion to a condemnation already pronounced, but more frequently the teaching is presented under the form of a positive explanation either by the popes and the bishops providing this teaching themselves or by their instructing someone else to do so. The acts of the ordinary magisterium are therefore varied and innumerable and take the form of Encyclicals, liturgical documents, sermons, Lenten pastoral letters, speeches, allocutions, censures, approbation given to books or catechisms, decisions of the Roman Congregations, etc. The sum total of these acts extending over the whole history of the Church constitutes the exercise of the ordinary magisterium.

But under what conditions does a particular doctrine enunciated by an act of the ordinary magisterium demand the assent of supernatural faith? Only if the ordinary magisterium infallibly proclaims that this particular doctrine is revealed by God. But how are we to know that the magisterium has made an infallible pronouncement? In fact none of the acts of the ordinary magisterium, considered in itself and in isolation, is infallible, whether it is a papal Encyclical or the placing of a book on the Index. How then are we to recognize that on any particular point the ordinary magisterium has made an infallible pronouncement? The answer is that the ordinary magisterium proposes teaching on faith and morals infallibly when it is unanimous in this teaching. It is sufficient moreover for this unanimity to be merely a moral one. In other words, the ordinary magisterium cannot err when it shows universal agreement about a given doctrine.

This, for example, is the case with the proposition "the Church is the Body of Christ". In isolation from the rest, none of the documents containing this assertion constitutes the infallible expression of the ordinary magisterium, even if it emanates from a pope like Boniface VIII. In fact, history shows that there is unanimity in all the acts of the ordinary magisterium that deal with this doctrine. Since this unanimity exists, we have to say that the ordinary magisterium infallibly teaches that the Church is the Body of Christ. This proposition is therefore a truth of faith.

Although the notion of the infallibility of the ordinary magisterium is in itself fairly simple, the identification of the cases in which the ordinary magisterium is exercised infallibly is somewhat less so. Let us suppose that a well-educated Christian is looking through Pius XII's Encyclical *Humani generis*, for instance, and that he reads the sentence which states that human reason can, absolutely speaking, reach a knowledge of a personal God. Let us suppose that the reader then asks himself what degree of assent he has in conscience to give to this proposition.

The character of the document will not enlighten him. An Encyclical, in fact, may contain teachings of very different value. Thus, our well-educated Christian will be well advised to consult on this point the Vatican Council which treated of this matter. But the Vatican Council, which "defined" that human reason is capable of knowing God, does not state in so many words that the knowledge in question is that of a *personal* God. In order to decide what degree of assent has to be given to the statement in the Encyclical *Humani generis* it would be necessary to investigate the whole corpus of the acts of the ordinary magisterium and to make certain that there is unanimity on this point. But it is not difficult to realize that only professional theologians can undertake such a task. And so our Christian left to himself will be unable to decide whether this proposition from *Humani generis* demands an assent of faith or only an inner intellectual adhesion.

Of course, anyone reading an Encyclical will be able to recognize in passing many truths of faith. But it is not certain that he will be able to do this in every case. Still less will he be able to tell in every case whether any given truth of faith (for example, the satisfaction for our sins which was made by Christ) has been taught by the extraordinary or the ordinary magisterium. True, the practical importance of this distinction is only secondary as far as the Christian life is concerned, since the only essential point is that we should know that a truth of faith is involved.

More complex cases may arise. Let us suppose that a Catholic scientist reads this other sentence in *Humani generis:* "We cannot at all see how this doctrine (the hypothesis according to which the human race is descended from several primitive couples, the hypothesis known as "polygenism") can be reconciled with the teaching on original sin put forward by the sources of revelation and the acts of the ecclesiastical magisterium." The scientist asks himself whether this statement asserts that faith and the polygenist hypothesis are incompatible. Certainly it does not do so directly, since the passage only says that we cannot see how to harmonize faith and the polygenist hypothesis. There is clearly a distinction here and it is an important one. But the layman, even if he is well-educated, cannot grasp the precise implication of this distinction. Only the professional theologian will succeed in doing so. And sometimes theologians themselves cannot reach complete agreement. This, in fact, is the case with the passage we are considering. In any event, however, these divergent views do not entitle us to regard the passage we have quoted as without force.

The practical consequence of all this is that it would be just as ridiculous to consider as infallible every word pronounced by a bishop or a pope even in a doctrinal matter as it would be out of the question to confine one's assent to definitions made by the Sovereign Pontiff or by an ecumenical Council. All teaching put forward by a pope or a bishop in the exercise of his duty, and out of loyalty to that duty, has a right at least to our respectful assent.

Some examples of doctrinal teaching

One difficulty cannot fail to suggest itself to our minds. Certain decisions of ecclesiastical authority, precisely because they demand our assent and obedience, have in fact delayed the spread of scientific and historical truths. This cannot be denied and the case of Galileo is the outstanding example. There are others also which are not so well known to the general public. Even though such cases as that of Galileo do not involve infallibility, people are disturbed and irritated by them. How can they continue to respect the authority of the Church when they consider facts such as these?

It must be regretfully admitted that at certain periods Churchmen have not been far-sighted enough to see beyond their own times and to understand that the scientific explanation of the revolution of the stars, for instance, has no essential connection with the truths of Revelation, and that certain discoveries are not opposed to Catholic doctrine—for example, that it is possible under certain conditions to understand the hypothesis of evolution in a Christian sense. Or again it may be regretted that the delay thus caused in the propagation of some truth should have damaged the Church's reputation in the eyes of men. At the same time, if we are to take a realistic view, we must modify our regret by taking into account what was and what was not possible at the time.

In any case, the essential mission of authority in the Church is not the advancement of science, even among theologians. Nor is its mission to provide a technical and adequate interpretation of the work of any given author when it refuses to accept his thought or condemns it. Its mission is to preserve the integrity of the faith and the fervour of charity in the Christian people, when certain doctrines oppose them. Thus authority rejects heterodox ideas as they are understood by the Christian people in the current circumstances or as they may easily be understood by people who are not capable of discrimination in such matters. This was the method used by the Council of Trent in the case of Luther. By acting in this way, the Church is faithful to her mission and fulfils the demands of Christian prudence, even though the prohibitions issued cause delay in the spread of certain hypotheses which the future will prove to have been correct (it may prove the exact opposite to be the case). The Church, we repeat, has not the duty of advancing science and scholarship, but the duty of leading the faith of the Christian people to the Truth. If certain statements of Loisy on revelation could not be understood or assimilated without danger to faith when Loisy was writing, then they had to wait. Later thought will show whether or not any given scientific innovation will have to be considered as a definitive truth. By insisting on delay in the teaching of these discoveries, even when they are in the sphere of religion, the Church is not failing in her essential mission. She is following a prudent course. It may well be that Churchmen have sometimes been too prudent or not intelligent enough. It must be allowed that these delaying tactics have sometimes been prompted in part by less honourable motives and considerations which were only too human. They have placed those whom they affected in extremely painful situations. All periods of the Church's history show examples of this.

But once we have admitted and deplored these facts, we still have to understand why the Church cannot and must not show a premature enthusiasm for human discoveries. What matters is that the truth which God himself has entrusted to the Church must not be corrupted. Eternity is of more importance than time; the fullness of truth is more important than any partial enlightenment.

Practical directives

The utterances of the pope and the bishops are not concerned only with statements about faith or morals. By virtue of the supernatural mission which our Lord has entrusted to her, the Church cannot fail to require that the temporal order should be established with justice and a justice which approximates increasingly to charity, the sovereign law of our existence. The Church therefore strives to bring the Christian virtues to bear on the affairs of the terrestrial city, to make them incarnate. Thus she would raise the level of temporal realities that they may become conditions favourable to the faith of Christians and the conversion of non-Christians. The Church cannot forget that God's will must be done "on earth as it is in heaven".

So the Church suggests and sometimes imposes directives in the field of action. At times she condemns and forbids certain activities. At other times, she encourages or earnestly exhorts her children. Thus from the nineteenth century onwards, as the industrial invasion modified the relations between man and man, the Church has intervened much more frequently, through her popes and bishops, in temporal affairs. We need only refer in this connection to protests against international violence, the approval given to aspirations for independence among colonial peoples, the warning uttered against premature nationalization, the assertion of the right to property under certain conditions. Many other instances could be quoted in the political, economic, social and international spheres.

Whatever form these interventions may take, the hierarchy makes them only in so far as Christian faith and morals are in question. The sole reason for these ecclesiastical directives can only be to direct the progress of the Christian people (and with them, the whole of mankind) towards our Lord with increased certainty and effectiveness. And this progress is threatened whenever a temporal order is established which directly opposes supernatural values or which rejects a purely natural value without directly attacking Christianity. To reject the indissolubility of marriage, or to deny the equality of the various human races, is to bar our access to supernatural realities. Submission to the natural order is a necessary condition if men are to hear the voice of the Holy Spirit. And it is certain that the institutions of a temporal order may paralyse men's consciences, stifle and deform them either through fear or through excess of well-being. In the presence of dangers such as these, in the presence of contempt for or ignorance of God's will, the Church cannot keep silent. She has to speak whenever she thinks that she can give advice useful in the conduct of human affairs. And who better than she can do this? She alone has a complete and disinterested knowledge of man and of his real destiny.

But these interventions in the temporal order are not the main function of the magisterium. As directives for concrete action they cannot be infallible. They nevertheless claim a respectful acceptance. They also demand obedience, if the Christian is in a position to take action, and in proportion to the gravity of the issues.

Necessary distinctions

Yet we must be careful not to "inflate" the governing authority.

Christian thought, as we have said, recognizes in ecclesiastical leaders the representatives of Christ. We must not conclude that the decisions of authority on any particular point are identical with the direct revelation of God's designs, as when Abraham heard God give him the order: "Go forth out of thy country." We must not claim that the decisions of the hierarchy are identical with those which Christ would make in similar circumstances. The members of the hierarchy are secondary causes. They remain so irremediably. They act with such intelligence, competence and skill as God has given them; he does not miraculously transform their imperfections into good qualities. He compensates for them (which is quite a different thing) by ways and means which we discern with difficulty or not at all. In spite of these insufficiencies, whether hidden or obvious, it is through such agents that Christ governs his Church. Through them he works out his plan of Redemption.

The true concept of obedience therefore does not consist in believing that every decision imposed by the hierarchy is the only possible one in the circumstances, the best in an absolute sense. We repeat, the Church's infallibility is only involved in the order of the magisterium and not at all in the purely jurisdictional order. No doubt the Holy Spirit assists the hierarchy to preserve it from blunders in its exercise of power. But the Holy Spirit has never promised to guarantee it against every blunder in the sphere of government. The possibility of erroneous decisions remains. Weakness and ignorance have been responsible for them. If the possibility of blunders does not affect our duty to obey, they will give rise to painful and difficult problems. There are famous instances in the past and in the present.

But one fact remains certain and sacrosanct. Nothing can shake it, not even the possibility of error: God wants us to obey his delegates when they give legitimate orders. The Son of God wrought the salvation of the world by his submission to his Father, sometimes directly, sometimes indirectly by his obedience to men and to human institutions. And since he made the Church his Body, he decreed that the obedience which began in the Head should continue in the Body, that in the Body as in the Head it should be redemptive obedience. Obedience is therefore integrated with the Church's very existence, it is a vital law in Christ's Body.

CONCLUSION

These reflections lead us to consider the activity and the humiliations of God in his Church.

Humanly speaking, it is absurd to claim that she has infallible authority when she proclaims a truth of faith. Only madness or pride would seem capable of accounting for such a claim. But time and misfortune have always overcome madness and pride. Twenty centuries have passed and they have certainly been twenty centuries of trouble for the Church. Faith in infallibility should have disappeared for infallibility is too heavy a responsibility for those who claim to exercise it and too hard to explain for those who are subject to it. If the disciples of any human master have ever accepted his infallibility, the belief has never lasted for long. It is to be noted that the Church gained nothing by proclaiming herself the mistress of infallible truth. It could not make her popular with the world, or with Christians separated from her.

Why, then, has not the Church abandoned it? The abandonment of any such claim by Protestantism and Anglicanism is significant. Humanly speaking, faith in infallibility and its permanence is almost impossible to explain. If it is not to be denied, all the power of the Holy Spirit is needed, we must have utter faith in Jesus Christ and his words. God's power alone can achieve this.

If God is the author of Catholic belief, his action nevertheless remains invisible, hidden beneath a human, an all too human, exterior. In the magisterium and in the exercise of jurisdiction, as in the Incarnation, the humiliation of the Son of God is manifested.

The Word of God is humiliated since the infallibility of the magisterium does not guarantee it against human limitations, against the inadequacy of words which are transcended by God's truth even when the sense proposed to our faith is infallibly and absolutely true. God's Word is humiliated because of the poverty of our human vocabulary, destined through it is to convey God's truth to the minds of men. And this poverty can never be overcome even when words are manipulated by theologians of genius.

There is a further humiliation, for our Lord did not promise his ministers, whether they are governing or teaching, a guarantee that they should receive the human talents necessary for a task which is utterly beyond them. Christ sought the leaders and the teachers of his Church on the lake of Genesareth and not in the schools or in the council chambers of kings. And the same is true today. The popes are not always brilliant personalities. Not all the bishops are clever, wise, learned or even saints. For one Augustine, there are so many who are quite undistinguished.

The real problem is always in the spiritual order. The point at issue is simply this, that we must remember in our own lives our Lord's words: "He who listens to you, listens to me." When Christ uttered these words, he knew what sort of men his disciples were, he knew the level of their intelligence and the limits of their generosity. Yet he said: "He who listens to you, listens to me."

We may well believe that, in the eyes of the world, the Church will always be "a little flock", not only small in numbers, in comparison with the mass of mankind, but small too in the means which she employs, in intelligence and in her visible triumphs. But above and beyond all her weaknesses, the revelation made to St Paul is still made to the whole Church, and faith alone can repeat the words in which he received it: "My grace is enough for thee; my strength finds its full scope in thy weakness" (2 Cor. 12. 9).

CHAPTER V

HOLY CHURCH, THE BODY OF CHRIST

"I believe in the *holy*, catholic Church." These words have been repeated by countless Christians through countless generations. As they utter them, these Christians of yesterday and of today declare that holiness is a mark of the Church, and so much so that where there is no holiness we know with complete certainty that there is no Church. This is tantamount to saying that holiness is part of the total mystery of the Church, that it is a visible and invisible element in her structure. Although we can indeed see it in part with the eyes of the body and those of the mind, we only genuinely grasp the whole truth concerning the Church's holiness through faith. But this act of faith, far from silencing questions, raises them.

We shall provisionally define holiness as the refusal to do what is morally evil in any shape or form. This being the case, we have to ask ourselves where this holy Church in which we believe is actually to be found. Is she in heaven among the elect? Will she begin to exist only at the end of time after the Last Judgement? Or does she exist here and now on our planet? In a word, is Holy Church something which we hope will appear in the world to come or is she an actual existing fact?

It was not long before people began to doubt whether the holiness of the Church was an existing reality. In the first centuries of the Church's life, the infant community called itself the assembly "of the saints" (Acts 9. 13; 26. 10, etc.). But some were of the opinion that this holy community was in fact far from justifying its claim or fulfilling its vocation. To improve their own lives, they considered they should live apart from the Church. Thus arose those of the Western heresies which presented the gravest dangers for the Church and their pretext was the lack of holiness among Christians. Well-known names occur in their history: Tertullian, Wyclif, Huss, Luther, Calvin. Mass movements form part of the story; of the Novatians in the third century, of the Donatists in the fourth and fifth, of the Waldensians in the thirteenth and Protestants in the sixteenth.

These events are very significant. The Catholic Church is reproached for not possessing a true understanding of holiness, or else for not being as holy as she ought to be. The latter complaint is considered decisive since it is argued that the Church must either be holy or cease to exist.

Yet Protestantism, apparently more modest than the Catholic Church, has ceased to assert that the Church must be holy in the strict sense of the term, and this is only logical. If man is a sinner and remains a sinner even when he has received the grace of justification, if sinful man is never intrinsically transformed by the grace of Jesus Christ, it seems impossible that we could use the word "holy" of the Church in an ontological sense applicable to her present situation. This does not mean that the Reformers ceased to declare that the Church is holy. But her holiness is given to her only in the "event" of the word, at the moment when Christ becomes present in preaching and in the sacrament (as understood by Protestant theology). Thus holiness remains extrinsic to the men who constitute the Christian assembly. It exists really in Christ alone and the Christian has no share in it. Holiness in the Church is therefore only a passing "event" such as the "event" of preaching. If holiness is spoken of in a definitive and permanent sense, this is only in the context of the last days and of the end of the world. The Church will be holy when all things have been accomplished. Since it is deferred in this way to the future, the holiness of the Church is no more than an object for which we hope.

John Huss taught that the Church was holy but in another sense. But he too maintained that holiness was above and beyond our experience but on the ground that only the elect predestined to see God constituted the holy Church. This is tantamount to saying that holiness remained "incognito" like the Church herself.

It would seem that in these ideas we encounter the spontaneous and unconscious resistance of the natural man. The latter feels an instinctive repugnance towards admitting that the supernatural order is linked to human realities and may inscribe itself upon them. Natural reason always protests when told that God has come down into this world, in whatever form. In other words what shocks the "secular" mind is the mystery of the Incarnation, its fulfilment in Jesus Christ or its continuation in the Church, in her activities, her existence and her holiness.

Moreover the natural man thinks that he has very good reasons for brushing the problem aside. Experience, he will say, makes it sufficiently clear that so-called holiness is pure imagination and that all claims to possess it are continually proved false. The Catholic, worried by these questions and uneasy before the tribunal of experience, is tempted, in his efforts to escape from his difficulty, to look on holiness as an ideal beyond this world. And so, dismayed by what he sees in the Church of history, this

Catholic begins to "platonize" and takes refuge in the contemplation of the "Idea" of the Church, an entity situated in an extra-historical realm. But by allowing himself to give way to this tendency, he is certainly jettisoning revealed truth. Pius XII complained about this in 1943 and quite recently an episcopal document echoed his protest as far as France is concerned (Pius XII, *Mystici Corporis*: Mgr Lefebvre, *Rapport doctrinal*, 1957).

THE CHURCH IS HOLY

If we are to speak realistically about the Church's holiness we must begin by looking once more at the material of which the Church is built.

By her rejection of the doctrine of John Huss, the Reformers and the Jansenists, the Church's magisterium repudiated those who, embarrassed by the visible, external Church, seek for a more genuine Church beyond the world. The fact is that, whether we like it or not, we must take the Church as our Lord made her, that is, as a people, organized, grouped and subject to the powers of order, of teaching and of government. The Church is not first and foremost in heaven, but on earth. The Church does not exist solely in the secret places of men's consciences, but lives also outside these consciences, in the market-place.

It cannot be otherwise since the Church is the assembly of men of flesh and bone, visibly united to one another through baptism, publicly professing the same faith and subject to the same leaders.

The Church of sinners

An important consequence follows from this truth. If membership of the Church depends solely, necessarily and adequately on baptism and the profession of the true faith, we must conclude that innocence is not an absolutely requisite condition for such membership and that the baptized will not be excluded from the Christian body for the sole reason that they are sinners, unless their sins are public and very grave. This is the teaching of Pius XII. He declared that those are truly members of the Church who are baptized and who profess the true faith, unless they have themselves broken away from the unity of the Body of Christ or have been cut off from it by legitimate authority for very serious misconduct (*Mystici Corporis*). Among such cases we must include those in which there is a public refusal to obey the Church and her head, the Vicar of Christ, or a public refusal to profess the Catholic faith. This is true also of public schism and heresy and of apostasy. Once this point has been made clear, we have to admit that a drunkard or a man guilty of adultery can remain in the Church. The Church *de facto* has no pretensions to be a "brotherhood of the pure", a class of people "who have nothing to reproach themselves with". She cannot make any such claim. She has within her walls sinners, very great sinners even, and she considers them as her children.

The Church had to do battle over a long period to preserve this somewhat inglorious tolerance. But the fight was necessary, for Scripture asserts that in the Kingdom of the Son of God there are scandals and that these will always exist (Matt. 13. 41; cf. 13. 47 *et seq*.). There can be no denying that this is a disagreeable truth and we should not easily accept it lightheartedly unless the Holy Spirit himself imposed it upon us as a duty. Moreover the Holy Spirit has taken the trouble to restate the same truth in other connections. Thus in the Apocalypse the letter to the seven Churches shows not only that there are sinners in the Church but that all the members of the Church are sinners to a greater or lesser degree (Apoc. 2. 5 *et seq*.; cf. 2 Thess. 2. 3). And St Paul's letters devote long passages to exhorting and reprimanding with considerable vehemence the sinners within the Church and to punishing them when necessary. The preaching of the Fathers of the Church often begins with the same sad fact that there are sinners in the Church and that they are there even though they are sinners. St John Chrysostom points a finger at the sinners in the Church and at their sins: "If it were possible", he writes, "to see men's souls laid bare, we should find in the Church, as in an army after a battle, that some are dead and others wounded. So then, I beg and pray you, let us lend one another a hand to rise again from sin."

There are then sinners in Christ's Church, there are even none who are not sinners. Doubtless, the more guilty of sin men are, the less do they effectively and genuinely belong to the Church. But they do belong to her all the same. Sinners are therefore within the Church, in spite of, yet with their sins. Although they can find nothing in the Church which justifies them in sinning, sinners live in the Church with their burden of sin (some refuse to accept this formula. Cf. Mgr Journet, *L'Église du Verbe Incarné*, II, pp. 913–14). It is at this point that the drama of the Church's holiness begins, for if it is certain that the sins of the baptized affect the Church though they do not, of course, destroy her, yet they do indeed affect her. (*Mystici Corporis* takes this for granted: *Quodsi in Ecclesia aliquid cernitur quod humanae arguit condicionis nostrae infirmitatem.*)

The Church of sinners is holy

We profess our faith precisely in the holiness of this Church which will be composed of sinners until the end of time: *Credo sanctam Ecclesiam. . . .*

This is the Catholic faith and it was spontaneously expressed from the beginning since it gave to the Church the title of the community of "saints" (Acts 9. 13, 32, 41; cf. Rom. 8. 27; 12. 13; 16. 2, etc.). But the apostles and the first Christians were not simple-minded men. They were well aware of the scandals in their company; there were Ananias and Saphira, the incestuous Corinthian and others. The Fathers of the Church in their turn were shrewd men but although they were inclined to castigate the sins of their flocks they were equally disposed to hymn the splendour of the Church. The Creeds, by incorporating the *Credo sanctam Ecclesiam* with the other articles, show what importance the Christian faith attaches to this truth. After the Creeds, the documents of the magisterium have repeated this same truth time after time and even when there was no occasion to do so. An evident fact emerges, namely, that holiness, according to Revelation, is not an accidental quality but an element in the very structure of the Church.

Catholics and Orthodox are unanimous on this point. That is why neither allow it to be said, as do some Protestants, that the Church has betrayed her trust. We do not doubt the good faith of these Protestants but we must absolutely reject this public accusation against the Church. And we shall now give the reason.

In the first place, let us concede the fact that the holiness of the Church, since it is affected by the sins of her members, always appears inadequate and imperfect. St John Chrysostom admitted this when he wrote: "The Church is a house built of our souls. And this house is not equally respectable in all its parts. Among the stones which go to make it up some are brilliant and polished whilst others are dark and of inferior quality but yet are better than some others." And so, we must admit that the holiness of the Church will never be fully achieved until the last day, when the purification of the members of the Body of Jesus Christ will be completed either by the trials endured on this earth or in the life beyond. In this respect the Church's holiness is eschatological. While she is still awaiting the end, she is incomplete, she lives in hope. When the end comes, then the universe will discover the beauty of the new City "like a bride who has adorned herself to meet her husband" (Apoc. 21. 2).

Nevertheless, here and now, the holiness of the Church is real. It is not simply a promise to be fulfilled in the life to come, it is a gift that has been genuinely granted and is possessed in the present. Further, it is not only an invisible holiness mysteriously hidden in men's hearts, it is holiness in some sense visible. As such the holiness of the Church is a possession that cannot be taken from her. It is all this which we have to understand and to justify.

THE SOURCE OF ALL HOLINESS IN THE CHURCH

The Church's holiness, both visible and invisible, has an invisible and inexhaustible source. If we are to identify the origin of this source, we must listen to the words of Revelation.

If we ask what is the source from which holiness flows unceasingly into the Church, the answer is obvious. The Church is the Body of Christ, and Jesus Christ is her Head. And the Head is holy and spotless. "Holiness is our Lord", says St Gregory of Nyssa (*In cant. canticorum*, Hom. XI, *P.G.* 44. 1108). If the Head is holy, how can the body fail to be so? St Augustine was well aware of this. He places the words of the Psalmist "I am holy" on the lips of Christ and then comments: "When Christ speaks in this way, he clearly speaks of his Body as well. . . . Then let the Body of Christ, let this one unique Man make bold to cry out from the ends of the earth and to declare with the Head and in union with the Head: 'I am holy'. If all the faithful who have been baptized in Jesus Christ have put on Christ, as the Apostle says, . . . if they have been made members of his Body and then say they are not holy members, they wrong the Head himself, for according to them his members are not holy.... See then where you stand and accept your own proper dignity from the Head" (*Enarratio in psalmum*, 85, 4, *P.L.* 37. 1084). We find the same idea in the writings of St Cyril of Alexandria: "The Church, drawn from all the nations, began to give her light for she possesses Christ in her sanctuary" (*De adoratione*, 10, *P.G.* 68. 657). In the case of St John Chrysostom, severity in regard to sinners does not silence his praise of "The House of the Church" in which "everything is made of gold and silver. There is the Body of Christ, there the Holy Virgin without spot or wrinkle" (*In secundam ep. ad Timotheum*, Hom. 6, No. 1, *P.G.* 62. 629). It is a pleasure to supplement these ancient Catholic statements by quoting the remarks of two Protestant pastors: "To say that the Church is holy is not to deny that sin is to be found in her, the sin, that is, of her members, even the sin of popes and bishops, it is to proclaim *the indissolubility of Christ's union with the Church.*" And the two authors add that "Catholicism takes the holiness of the Church very seriously" (quoted by Fr Villain, *Introduction à l'Écuménisme*, 1958, p. 132).

This quotation does justice to Catholic thought. Union and holiness; these are two interdependent truths. And once we know why and how the union of Christ and the Church is achieved and maintained, we immediately become aware of how holiness in the Church is achieved and maintained.

The union of Christ and the Church is forged at both the institutional and the spiritual levels. By the *institutional* level we mean the mission entrusted to the Church, the structure which she has been given by Christ, the juridical links between Christ and the Church which have been established by the conferring of the mission and of the three powers. This institutional level is not merely juridical if by this term we imply that the Church's institution is no more than a kind of "order in Council" unconnected with the nature of the Church as such; it is an ontological level, that is, it affects the very being of the Church and so merges into the spiritual order and, as we shall see, enriches it.

The *spiritual* level is, in the strict sense, the inner transformation of the souls of men which, to the extent that God allows, becomes conformed to the image of the Son of God. The spiritual is a moral level, yet it is more than a moral level, it is supernatural and makes us like Christ himself. It is ontological in the full sense of the word, for here holiness is inscribed upon the soul, raises it up, makes it divine, makes it "share in the divine nature". It is the order of grace properly so called in which the life of the Son of God becomes truly the life of man.

We may say that the institutional level constitutes the *objective* order of holiness, and the spiritual level its *subjective* order. Whatever term we use, the fact remains that the two types of holiness are different. Under these two aspects, both *invisible* to us, the holiness of the Church will never fail, and it therefore follows that its *visible* radiance also will never fail. In other words the history of the Catholic Church will always have its saints, whether canonized or not, whether they are worthy or not to be remembered by the generations to come, whether or not their holiness is visible.

PERPETUAL AND INVISIBLE HOLINESS

There is therefore in the Church an invisible holiness. It is perpetual as the union of Christ and the Church is perpetual. It is found at various levels, but in all of these the mystery of the Church is made manifest.

Objective and institutional holiness

The *Catholica*, independently of the virtues of each individual Christian and in spite of the deficiencies of them all, is holy because she belongs to Christ, she is his domain, his Bride. The latter image is found in Scripture, and it gives us the best idea of objective holiness. The bond of wedlock implies on the one hand the juridical and institutional aspect, and on the other it points to the spiritual order, to the union of souls. The image also clarifies the meaning of objective holiness. Just as the wife shares in the dignity of her husband through the marriage bond and deserves respect because of her husband's qualities, so the Church, since she is linked with Christ, shares in the sovereign splendour of Jesus Christ. It is no mean thing to be for ever united to our Lord.

Let there be no misunderstanding on this point; we are not concerned here with holiness in the moral sense, that is, with the rejection of sin. We are concerned with holiness in a physical sense, and its appropriate name is "holiness by consecration". The following comparison will help us to grasp the meaning of the phrase. The blessing given to objects used for worship effects no change in the value of the matter of which they are composed, gold, silver, tin or wood. But we say that they are "holy", and not without reason. They cease to be like other objects. They are distinguished from these by the use to which they are put. They become holy because of the purpose for which they are used, namely to honour and praise the divine Majesty through the agency of men. No doubt holiness in this sense is of a very lowly kind, it is the holiness of things, of objects. The worth of the holy picture or the chalice does not lie so much in themselves as in their use for public worship and in the religious intention of the man who consecrates them. And these seem to belong to these objects and to exist in them. The same is true of the Church. The bond by which the Church is consecrated to Christ has its origin in our Lord. He gradually forged it and finally established it during his life on earth.

Yet this bond of union is not simply in the past and without any relevance to the present. Although it is certainly a juridical "ligament", it is not inert. Christ continues to give reality to the institutional links between his Church and himself. Whenever baptism is administered, our Lord accomplishes this task and in the ears of the baptized person the summons to his Church and her mission rings out anew. More than this, Church and mission are inscribed upon the spiritual nature of the baptized person like a seal in wax and they constitute the foundations of his being as a Christian. Thus Christ raises the baptized to the dignity of membership in his Body and at the same time introduces them to the holiness of membership and of consecration. This "event" is known as the sacramental character.

We still need to understand what is meant by this consecration and this holiness conferred by Christ with the sacramental character. These abundant gifts do not exist in us like a jewel inside a case. Our consecration and our membership continue solely because our Lord, faithful to his promises, ceaselessly obtains them for and preserves them in us. Our Lord keeps unfailing faith with us, he will never go back on his word, he will not cast doubt on our membership and consecration; of this we can be certain, but it is his faithfulness to his promises that alone guarantees it. Thus every man, even the worst of criminals, as soon as he has answered this summons and received this consecration, enters into a definitive possession of "institutional" holiness. Whatever the spiritual quality of the baptized man, his consecration destines him for a higher service than that of worldly and ephemeral interests, it assigns him a task in the plan of Redemption.

This then is the institutional and objective holiness of the Church. It is the holiness of our election and consecration. To say this is not an abuse of language. Once our Lord's call comes to men, it does not remain outside those it reaches. It grafts itself on to their spiritual substance, and imprints a definitive character upon it. This is why sacramental character is the holiness deriving from our vocation and consecration. Through this character, each of us is included in the call, each of us is subject to the demands and to the mission of the Church, each of us lies open to the grace which makes it possible for him to be faithful to these demands and to this mission.

We are now treating of the source of all spiritual riches. And it is a juridical link by which every Christian receives his share in the consecration which Christ himself has received. Hence it is an over-simplification to set the juridical aspect of the realities of the Church's existence over against the supernatural values, since the outpouring of God's gifts is inseparable from the fact of institution, from the transference of Christ's consecration to the Church and her members (*Mystici Corporis*).

This objective and institutional holiness is indestructible. Even if the impossible should happen and all the Christians in the Church were to be in a state of mortal sin, we should still have to say that the Church is holy because this bond of consecration links her for ever to Christ. It will always be true that the Church is the people which the Son of God has willed should exist and has established as his chosen and consecrated people. Finally, this holiness is *immutable*. It does not depend on the virtue and merits of individuals but solely on our Lord's own decision, on his choice, on the mission which he has entrusted to the Church. Like the will of our Lord himself it cannot change.

Subjective holiness and transfiguration

Jesus would not be the true Head of his Church, according to Revelation, if he conferred upon her the holiness of election and consecration alone. Great as this is, the holiness which Christ has willed his Church to possess is of a yet higher kind.

The fact is that it is nothing less than the Son of God's own life. "In Christ is the fullness of all graces", declares St Thomas. Therefore Jesus "possesses the power to pour out his grace on all the members of the Church according to the words of John: 'We have all received something out of his abundance'." And St Thomas adds, "from Christ our Head spiritual impulses and life pour out upon all the members of the Church" (*In epistolam primam ad Corinthios,* cap. XI, *lectio prima; Summa theologica,* 3a Pars, qu. 8, art. 1).

The holiness we are now considering includes moral purity and light; it goes without saying that it implies a refusal of all sin. But it is much more than all this, it is man's assimilation into Christ and it becomes a communion with God himself. In a word, Catholic holiness is a transfiguration which makes us divine since the Son of God grants us his own personal life. It is true that we are here in the presence of a reality beyond our experience, beyond all the familiar, natural universe. Although it is possible to have some idea of a man's moral worth it is impossible to measure his union with God, to perceive it behind his defects, the limits of his temperament, his sins even, and to recognize with absolute certainty the presence or the absence of the grace which makes us divine. It is impossible even fully to understand what is meant by the expressions "a transfiguration that makes us divine", or "a share in the divine nature". Here, the majesty of the Church disappears into mystery; it escapes us, even though it has been revealed to us by God.

Yet it is possible to describe the holiness of union and transfiguration. It penetrates the different levels of the human soul; on the one hand, it raises the faculties to a higher state, on the other, it impregnates the soul's very essence.

Union with God and transfiguration begin when man's spirit is drawn towards the truth of God and recognizes in Jesus Christ the Lord and Creator of the universe. God himself then becomes for the believing intelligence the faithful witness, the guarantor of the articles of the Creed. This is faith, the union of the human intelligence with the uncreated Light. To have faith is therefore to have access to holiness by opening ourselves to the teaching of the Father. When the believer accepts Christ, the Master of Wisdom, he accepts with Christ the true and most holy light. Henceforth as he looks at the world, the Church and Christ, with the light God gives him, the faithful soul has access to the holiness of God through the gates of knowledge.

Yet holiness works a still deeper transfiguration in our spiritual being. It can so transfigure it that it kindles in it a flame of infinite charity. In the prayer before his arrest, our Lord asked that the Church should possess that holiness which is union and charity. It is so transcendent, so divine, that it can only be compared to the union of the Father and the Son in the Blessed Trinity: "that they may all be one, Father . . . as thou art in me, and I in thee" (John 17. 21–3; 17. 11). Further, the holiness of union between men is achieved not apart from and, as it were, at a distance from, but within God himself: "that they too may be one in us". our Lord again asked, "that while thou art in me, I may be in them, and so they may be perfectly made one" (John 17. 21–3). Thus the holiness of the Church, her most profoundly Christian holiness, exists in and by that unifying Love which God himself is. It is a participation in divine Love. And this is precisely what Christ asked for in his final petition: *"that the love thou hast bestowed upon me may dwell in them"* (John 17. 26).

The abundance of riches promised to the Church is foretold by Christ in yet another way. The language which he uses is indeed mysterious but we cannot brush it aside merely because it is mysterious. His own words are: "If a man has any love for me, he will be true to my word; and then he will win my Father's love, and we will both come to him, and *make our continual abode with him*" (John 14. 23). This statement was already implicit in the passages already quoted. But now everything is clear. The holiness offered to the Christian is that whereby he becomes a temple of God.

This holiness is the vocation of every Christian; it is not reserved for a few privileged souls. Thus the Church is holy because in her our Lord transfigures men of goodwill, remains in them as in a sanctuary, conforms them to the image of the Son of God, raises them to the rank of heirs of God and co-heirs with Christ (Rom. 8. 29; 8. 17).

Our Lord is faithful to his word. As he consecrated the bread that it might become his body, so also does he permanently consecrate his Church that she may be his mystical Body. This act of consecration cannot be less efficacious than that of the Last Supper. No doubt, each Christian may fail and may desecrate in himself the holiness which he has received from our Lord. But the whole Church cannot fail because Christ's gesture of consecration will always give birth in the Church to faith, to hope and to charity, that is, to supernatural holiness.

Union and transfiguration—these are *imperishable* in the Church, but they are *mutable*. They ebb and flow according to the rhythms of human liberty. Institutional and objective holiness is absolutely independent of man's goodwill, but the holiness of transfiguration depends upon the dispositions of the baptized. It varies according as the Christian people corresponds or fails to correspond to the inspirations of the Holy Spirit.

THE VISIBLE AND CONTINUAL MANIFESTATION OF THE CHURCH'S HOLINESS

An essential characteristic of the Church's holiness is its visible manifestation. This needs to be explicitly stated if we are to do justice to the mystery of the Church. This mystery is a divine reality and the work of God, yet present under outward and human appearances. The moving patterns of history both reveal and at the same time obscure it. This is true also of the Church's holiness.

Visible holiness is essential to the Church

The most convenient way of dealing with this subject would be to pass it by without more ado. Merely to touch on it exposes us very obviously to objections. It is so easy to point out deficiencies in the treatment of this particular matter.

But we cannot possibly omit the problem. Christ himself showed far too clearly that visible holiness is of the nature of the Church for it to be possible to pretend to ignore it. "It was not you that chose me", he said to his apostles, "it was I that chose you. The task I have appointed you is to go out and bear fruit, fruit which will endure" (John 15. 16). Can this fruit be hidden? This could not possibly be, for Christ elsewhere declares that the good fruit makes known the good tree (Matt. 17. 17–20). Moreover our Lord made his teaching clearer still when he spoke of charity: "The mark by which all men will know you for my disciples will be the love you bear one another" (John 13. 35). Finally, in the prayer that followed the Last Supper, Christ asked that the holy union between the members of the Church should be a sign to the world of the truth of his mission: "that they too may be one in us . . . so that the world may come to believe that it is thou who hast sent me" (John 17. 21; 17. 23).

Since holiness is Jesus Christ's own life in man, how can we suppose that our Lord's life is inert, that it fails to shine forth or is mute and inactive? The Vatican Council is only expressing the teaching of Scripture and the sense of the faithful when it declares: "The Church in herself, *by reason* of her admirable diffusion throughout the world and *her eminent holiness,* . . . is a decisive and continual motive of credibility and bears indisputable witness to her divine mission" (Denz. 1794).

The Church could not be unaware that such a declaration provoked her opponents and exposed her to criticisms that are only too easily made. If, in spite of this, she has spoken in this way, it is because revelation makes it her duty to do so.

The identification of holiness

We must first remind the reader that we cannot establish the fact of holiness as a policeman takes note of a street accident. Holiness is a spiritual value and no spiritual value can be observed if the mind is insensitive to this value. The beauty of music can only be sensed if one is to some extent a musician oneself. The same is true of our perception of the value represented by holiness. Only the man who has a grain of it, however small, within himself, only the man who has a longing, however feeble, for a spirit of disinterestedness and of sacrifice, can become aware of its presence. If this is lacking, the presence of holiness completely escapes him. Unable as he is to decipher the signs in which virtue finds expression, the man who has no feeling for moral values discovers around him nothing but mean and selfish purposes. The identification of holiness is inseparable from the personal problem and inevitably depends on the spiritual attitude of the spectator.

The outward appearances of the Church's holiness

If Christian holiness is to be understood, there are other common misconceptions to be removed. Otherwise demands will be made with which the Church cannot comply.

Some comparisons are in fact unfortunate. The Church's holiness is in no way identical with philanthropy; it is not anthropocentric but theocentric. It puts things in their right order; we are to love God and serve him with all our mind, heart and strength, and then our neighbour is to be loved as he should be, that is in relation to his true interests as a son of God. The Church's holiness would not be the holiness of Jesus Christ unless she proclaimed the absolute sovereignty and primacy of the Most High and the Most Holy. Hence the Church's holiness can never be reduced to the meagre proportions of any social utilitarianism. For many people, this will be an unintelligible and unpardonable defect and they will be unable to see the splendour of the Church.

Nor must holiness be confused with "perfection" as understood by the wise men of antiquity. They did everything within the exact limits defined by reason. The wise man speaks when it is necessary, keeps silent when it is necessary, laughs in moderation, acts at all times and in all places as the occasion demands. But holiness in the Church's sense is not confined to this sort of conduct. To be correct in one's behaviour is not the saint's principal preoccupation, as though the problem were appropriately solved when everybody says, "There's nothing wrong with him". It is understandable, since this is so, that the Church's holiness certainly does not provide a good line in propaganda. It promises nothing spectacular. It is not in the same class as moral "endeavour" or Spartan heroism. The life of Christ in men's souls does not transform their temperaments; it usually leaves them to struggle with their congenital laziness or violence, it does not suppress the defects or hereditary influences. As a general rule, the holiness of the Christian performs no miracle as far as his nature is concerned. This is why, when we consider any particular individual, it is never possible to identify infallibly the existence of the grace of Jesus Christ or the presence of holiness in him.

In actual fact, the holiness proper to the Church begins when a man, to however small a degree, understands and subscribes to the infinite demands of the Christian vocation: "Be perfect as your heavenly Father is perfect." As soon as a baptized person recognizes, explicitly or implicitly, that this principle is the law of his own personal existence, there is at least a beginning of holiness in him. The Protestant Kierkegaard saw clearly that an essential truth was involved at this point: "We must not soft-pedal the demands (of Christianity) we must increase them. . . . Wherever God enters into the picture, true progress will be recognized by the fact that there is an increase in the demands that are made, by the fact that life has become more difficult." Hence he saw in the suppression of monasticism one reason for doubt about the justice of the Lutheran cause. There are, of course, various ways of putting the precept of perfection into practice. There is the heroic way: "We too must be ready to lay down our lives for the sake of our brethren" (1 John 3. 16). There is the ordinary way: we do our duty day by day, realizing that we can always do better: "when you have done all that was commanded you, you are to say, We are servants and worthless; it was our duty to do what we have done" (Luke 16. 10).

This phrase of our Lord's is profoundly significant. It leads us to another aspect of holiness, namely, humility. Far from being the least in importance, it is in fact fundamental. The Church's holiness is not equivalent to impeccability and she is fully aware of this. She knows, and with her all Christians know, that men are sinners. Every morning and evening and at every Mass, the Church confesses the sins of her members as she says the *Confiteor* and the Lord's Prayer. The Church's holiness therefore is neither triumphant nor glorious, it is not even sure of itself. The holiness of the Body of Christ can only be genuine on condition that the members of the Body admit the evil that they have done and their instinctive and constant complicity in all moral evil. In this respect, the Church is holy because she admits that she is not as holy as she ought to be, and she demands that each of her children should recognize this fact publicly by going to confession at least once a year. Worthy people do not greatly admire the Church for this sort of humility. Most men see the sin and not the humility, and even if they do see it they are not much impressed. St Augustine understood the unique character of the Church's humility when he wrote: "It is not found in any of the books of the sects outside the Church, it is not found among the Manicheans, nor among the Platonists, nor among the Epicureans and the Stoics. Even where the best precepts and teaching are available, humility is not to be found. The way of humility has its origins elsewhere, in Christ." Nothing could be more true. Humility is the sign that distinguishes the holiness of the Church. Where it is lacking, there is no Christian virtue. "Unless . . . you become like little children . . ." (Matt. 18. 3). Thus the only human society which is on the road to holiness is that which confesses its sins. There is no need to ask where this human society is to be found, whether the majority of its members are in the Church or elsewhere.

Where there is humility, holiness becomes possible, for charity can exist. We must believe St Augustine when he insists that the edifice of spiritual perfection will rise all the higher in proportion as we have dug more deeply, with humility as its foundations. Charity is only possible if we consent to complete self-effacement.

Charity has a thousand forms. It cannot be reduced simply to the help which we give to men struggling with material problems. There are less glorious acts of charity, yet they are just as necessary; patience, for example. Does not holiness also consist in putting up with things, in waiting, in marking time, in refusing to force the pace of events?

This is a very sore point with some who would often find it easier to forgive virtue for being intolerant. It appears under such circumstances in a more advantageous light. It is no doubt true that charity has sometimes to be violent and take Christ's whip to drive away the buyers and sellers from the Temple. But this was an unusual event in Christ's life and it must be unusual also in the life of the Church. Our daily duty is of a different kind. It consists in meeting sinners, in sitting down at their table, in being in the world with other people whoever they may be. This causes the Pharisees to take scandal, and the weak too. They would like the Church to protest, to organize demonstrations, to reject, to excommunicate, to behave dramatically. But they are wrong. It is because the Church is holy like Christ that she has to be patient.

Thus the Church tolerates sinners within her walls and she will continue to tolerate them. She gives them her message and she will go on giving it to them. She will only cease to do so if there is grave, public scandal involved. Not that the Church has any need of sinners. On the contrary, they are a decided embarrassment to her. But sinners need the Church and charity imposes on her the duty of not ignoring them, of not brushing them to one side by so ignoring them. As long as the Church has reason to suppose that there is still some trace of good intentions, some repentance, she continues to abide by that supposition. She does not decide to drive away those who have been baptized, to refuse them the sacraments and Christian burial, unless it is no longer possible to do otherwise. There is a form of holiness which would be easy, too easy. It would insist on "purity" in the secular sense, that is, it would avoid all compromise and all risk of compromising itself, by refusing to have any contact with sinners. Did our Lord ever act like this? No, he preferred to risk being misunderstood and criticized rather than to allow one single sinner to look for him without finding him. The Church must act as did her Head.

Aspects of holiness

The holiness of the Church clearly manifests itself in history. It does so primarily and essentially as an ever-present demand that Christians should be perfect. The religious life throughout the centuries is a proof of this. The fact that it exists continues to be an astonishing phenomenon. In this widespread institutional form it has no equivalent outside Christianity. Far from disappearing in the course of time, it shows a tendency to invade states of life which might well seem strangers to it. Thus the priestly life and the life of the laity in the world are gradually incorporating elements of the religious life. In the obligations imposed on priests and on members of Secular Institutes, it is always the desire for perfection which finds expression. Quite recently, important and reiterated enactments of Pius XII were directed to the encouragement of the religious life in the Church. Greco-Russian Orthodoxy has not abandoned this form of Christian life and holiness. Luther did away with it along with many other things and it was only in the nineteenth century that Anglicanism resumed contact with the monastic tradition. Protestants have begun a discreet and preliminary return to the religious life during the past few years. So true it is that the religious life is an accurate expression of the indefeasible demands of Christian holiness.

But every spiritual impulse grows exhausted in the very process of its movement, the more so as it is the more spiritual and the more exacting. The life of the Church could not escape the working of this law. Nevertheless, it is a striking fact that the Church ensures her own rejuvenation through successive internal reforms. Thus we see Gregory VII struggling to safeguard the purity of the Church's mission in a world which was attempting to secularize it, St Francis of Assisi preaching poverty, St Dominic founding the Order of Preachers. The Council of Trent (1545–63) was an attempt at spiritual and institutional reform on a scale that has no parallel. St Ignatius Loyola took his modest share in this by devoting to it his society of priests. The seventeenth century was in its turn to see a spiritual revival made illustrious by the names of Francis de Sales, Vincent de Paul and Marie de l'Incarnation. It would be easy to continue the list of facts down to our own time.

In another and more limited sphere, that of sexual morality, the Church maintains the constant rigour of her demands. She alone continues to do so in spite of enormous pressure from public opinion and from governments, in spite even of the sins her own children commit in this domain. As regards conjugal morality, divorce, abortion, and so forth, the Church has not yielded, even at the risk of appearing unreasonable. Never for one moment do we find her choosing the easy way out. The Church undertakes to defend man against himself. If, in the past, she has had to exercise charity towards men by teaching them to read and write, by taking care of the sick when no one else came forward to do so, today the exercise of charity takes on another and more difficult form. Nowadays it is the degradation of the human person which has to be prevented and the transformation of human beings into instruments at the service of eugenics, science, or some other idol or, worse still, of their own instincts when they become their slaves. The holiness of the Church is put to the test. It would be easy to moderate her demands in the interests of peace. If we compare her attitude with that of other Christian bodies we soon see that her firm stand is significant.

These brief allusions are sufficient for our purpose: the Body of Christ has not failed; today as yesterday it bears witness to the infinite scope of the Christian vocation. It bears witness to it in very humble ways for most of the time; men must repent, they must keep on beginning all over again, they must not lower their standard even when faithfulness to it costs dear, even when the Christian finds that he is far below the ideal and stands condemned by it.

Those who throughout history have upheld this vocation have been sinners. Their temptation must have been to bring principles down to the level of practice, to justify their own weaknesses by abandoning principles which were too far above them. It did not win the day. A power from beyond the world has entered it.

SACRAMENTAL HOLINESS

The faithfulness of the Church is rooted in Jesus Christ and his sacraments. The source of even the most ordinary supernatural virtue is not the product of our unaided liberty. Holiness is not essentially the fruit of an intellectual or moral asceticism. We may go still further and say that it is not the reward of a prayer offered to God by man using only his powers as a man.

Whether it be the holiness of consecration or the holiness of transfiguration, nothing comes from man as though he were its author: "What powers hast thou, that did not come to thee by gift?" (1 Cor. 4. 7). The holiness of consecration is imprinted solely by the sacramental character received in baptism, confirmation and holy order. The very fact that nobody can administer these sacraments to himself is the sign of the radical powerlessness of man to acquire supernatural holiness. The holiness of transfiguration also only comes to us through the sacraments. Just as there is no salvation without the Church, so there is no holiness without the Church and the Church's sacraments. Their primordial source is the Eucharist. It could not be otherwise since in Eucharistic communion the faithful, as St Cyril of Jerusalem realistically says, become "of one body and of one blood" with Christ. Hence it is the consummation of every spiritual life and the source of all holiness (*Summa Theol.*, 3a Pars, q. 79, art. 6; cf. q. 73, art. 3; q. 79, art. 1 ad 1).

Thus the sacraments are object lessons. They teach us both that Christ accomplishes the work of sanctification by himself alone and also that he does not accomplish it without some gesture of acceptance on our part. "Be perfect as your heavenly Father is perfect", says Jesus. But it is impossible since "separated from me, you have no power to do anything" (John 15. 5). St Paul provides the answer to the riddle when he writes: "nothing is beyond my powers, thanks to the strength God gives me" (Phil. 4. 13).

CONCLUSION

The holiness of the Church cannot be appreciated at its true value, if we discern in it only the virtue of individual Christians. In fact, the holiness of the Body of Christ is that of a great mass of men. Each Christian, for his own part, adds his note to the symphony, a virtue he possesses, repentance for his sins, the desire to pull himself together again after a fall. Every baptized person enriches the whole by his own temperament, his own generosity, none of them is a complete expression of it.

Let us then look at the mass of Christians and its age-old history. Here and there we see lights emerge. Some are brilliant, very brilliant even, but they are as rare as the lamps in a tunnel. Yet they are sufficient for the mass to be guided by their light. The great multitude limps along, but it is on the move all the same. We have to realize that this people continues to go forward. There is a small compact nucleus; the others follow in a disorderly fashion and as well as they can, but they do follow. We must also take note of the strange power which enables the Church to rise up once more after sinking into the most sombre and least holy periods in her history. Then we shall understand what the words "holy Church" mean.

This vision at the same time reveals how the Incarnate Word humbles himself in the Church. The sovereign purity of God has "emptied" itself by taking our human condition in Jesus of Nazareth (Phil. 2. 7). The Most Holy humbles himself anew and at a lower level still by taking upon himself the condition of the mass of humanity. The holiness of God in Jesus Christ did not escape the breath of scandal since it was made manifest in human form. Christ was called a glutton and a lover of wine when he was found at the table of publicans and sinners (Matt. 11. 19). Still less can the holiness of the Church escape the breath of scandal. Christ himself could confound his opponents by putting to them the question: "Which of you shall convince me of sin?" The Church cannot. The Church's virtues are those of a mass of sinners, whose only inalienable privilege is that they can confess their sins, their powerlessness and their weakness in the presence of the demands of their calling. Thus the humiliation which Christ's holiness suffers is more profound in the Church than in the Incarnation. It is a greater test of the faith of believers, it is more dangerous for the unbelief of others.

Yet the words of Jesus do not pass away. They are as true for us as they were for Judas: "Blessed is he who shall not be scandalized in me" and because of my Church.

CONCLUSION

To the historian contemplating the passage of the centuries, the Church is so involved in the history of mankind that it is only with great difficulty that one can be distinguished from the other. It is a fact that human appearances are similar in both; and all historical phenomena are like one another precisely because they are historical phenomena. But in reality the eye of faith perceives the supernatural substance of this history. And it is the mystery of the Incarnation and passion of Jesus Christ continuously present in the universe and in its evolution, through and in the Church. To passing events that have soon disappeared from the scene, the Church brings a value that cannot perish, she transforms them into "riches for eternity", because in her as in Jesus Christ, the Incarnation (presence in the world) and the passion (separation from the world) are daily changed into resurrection. It is through the Church that we await this resurrection at the time God has determined.

"Your life is hidden away now with Christ in God. Christ is your life, and when he is made manifest, you too will be made manifest in glory with him" (Col. 3. 3–4). Yet here and now, the pledge of the resurrection is given to all those who, day by day and hour by hour, remain faithful to the call of the Incarnation and the cross: "How rich is God in mercy, with what an excess of love he loved us. . . . *He, in giving life to Christ, gave life to us too . . . raised us up too, enthroned us above the heavens,* in Christ Jesus" (Ephes. 2. 4–6). It is therefore an accomplished fact; the Church here and now shares invisibly in Christ's glorious resurrection while she goes forward visibly upon this earth. It could not be otherwise for "(Jesus) is risen already. Our Head is therefore in heaven. Where the Head is, thither go the members" (St Augustine, *Sermo* 1371, *P.L.* 38. 754).

Thus the Church journeys through time, "Christ Jesus has won the mastery over" her and she "presses on" (Phil. 3. 12, 16). The Church is obedient to the ideal of the Christian life as described by St Paul for the benefit of the Philippians. She has only to accept the mysteries of our Lord, to make them her own both on earth and in heaven, as did the Apostle himself, who was the model of the Church's life:

> Forgetting what I have left behind, intent on what lies before me, I press on with the goal in view.
>
> Him I would learn to know, and the virtue of his resurrection, and what it means to share his sufferings, moulded into the pattern of his death.
>
> We find our true home in heaven. It is to heaven that we look expectantly for the coming of our Lord Jesus Christ to save us; he will form this humbled body of ours anew, moulding it into the image of his glorified body (Phil. 3).

True history is enacted in and by the Church at this price and only at this price. In the Body of Christ, and through it, real history is made and it is not merely political conflict or economic competition. In and through the Body of Christ, duration reaches its transcendent term, time passes into eternity, that which is passing is changed into that which remains for ever. Thus, and there is surely no need to repeat it, the true human race dreamed of by the imaginations of good people and by those of the builders of empires, is not brought into existence merely in earthly civilizations and by political institutions, but first and essentially at that place and time when the people of God began to appear, where the Body of Christ now dwells, wherever men gather together in the shadow of the Church and of her mystery.

SELECT BIBLIOGRAPHY

In this series:

D'ORMESSON, Wladimir: *The Papacy*; RÉTIF, André, S.J.: *The Catholic Spirit.*

ADAM, Karl: *The Spirit of Catholicism*, London, Sheed and Ward, 1938, and Washington, D.C., Pantheon, 1954; *One and Holy*, London and New York, Sheed and Ward, 1954.

CERFAUX, L.: *Theology of the Church in St Paul*, London and New York, Herder-Nelson, 1959.

CLÉRISSAC, Yves, O.P.: *The Mystery of the Church*, London, Sheed and Ward, 1937.

CONGAR, Yves M. J.: *Christ, Our Lady and the Church*, London, Longmans, and Westminster, Md, Newman Press, 1957; *Mystery of the Church*, London, Geoffrey Chapman, and Baltimore, Helicon Press, 1960; *Lay People in the Church*, 2nd edn, London, Geoffrey Chapman, 1960, and Westminster, Md, Newman Press, 1957.

D'ARCY, M. C., S.J.: *The Life of the Church*, London, Sheed and Ward, 1932.

GRABOWSKI, Stanislaus J.: *The Church*, St Louis, Mo., Herder, 1958.

HASSEVELDT, Roger: *The Church, a Divine Mystery*, Chicago, Fides, 1957.

JOURNET, Charles: *The Church of the Word Incarnate*, London and New York, Sheed and Ward, 1955.

MONTCHEUIL, Yves de: *Aspects of the Church*, Chicago, Fides, 1955.

SCHEEBEN, Matthias: *Mysteries of Christianity*, St Louis, Mo., Herder, 1946.

The papal Encyclicals quoted in the text may be consulted in: FREMANTLE, Anne: *Papal Encyclicals in their Historical Context*, New York, Putnam, 1956. Single Encyclicals are published in English by the Catholic Truth Society of London and by the N.C.W.C. of Washington, D.C.

The Twentieth Century Encyclopedia of Catholicism

The number of each volume indicates its place in the over-all series and not the order of publication.

PART ONE: KNOWLEDGE AND FAITH

1. What Does Man Know?
2. Is Theology a Science?
3. The Meaning of Tradition
4. The Foundations of Faith
5. Do Dogmas Change?
6. What is Faith?
7. God's Word to Man
8. Myth or Mystery?
9. What is a Miracle?
10. Is There a Christian Philosophy?
11. Early Christian Philosophy
12. Medieval Christian Philosophy
13. The Basis of Belief
14. Does Christianity Oppose Science?
15. The God of Reason

PART TWO: THE BASIC TRUTHS

16. The Worship of God
17. What is the Trinity?
18. The Holy Spirit
19. In the Hands of the Creator
20. The Problem of Evil
21. Who is the Devil?
22. Freedom and Providence
23. The Theology of Grace
24. The Incarnation
25. What is Redemption?
26. The Communion of Saints
27. Faith, Hope and Charity
28. Life After Death

PART THREE: THE NATURE OF MAN

29. The Origins of Man
30. Evolution
31. What is Man?
32. What is Life?
33. What is Psychology?
34. Man in His Environment
35. Man and Metaphysics
36. Psychical Phenomena

PART FOUR: THE MEANS OF REDEMPTION

37. Prayer
38. The Nature of Mysticism
39. Spiritual Writers of the Early Church
40. Spiritual Writers of the Middle Ages
41. Post-Reformation Spirituality
42. Spirituality in Modern Times
43. What are Indulgences?
44. Mary The Mother of God
45. The Marian Cult
46. What is a Saint?
47. What is an Angel?

PART FIVE: THE LIFE OF FAITH

48. What is the Church?
49. What is a Sacrament?
50. Christian Initiation
51. Penance and Absolution
52. What is the Eucharist?
53. What is a Priest?
54. Christian Marriage
55. Death and the Christian
56. Christian Morality
57. Christian Social Teaching
58. World Morality
59. Christianity and Money

PART SIX: THE WORD OF GOD

60. What is the Bible?
61. The Promised Land
62. Biblical Archaeology
63. Biblical Criticism
64. God's People in the Bible
65. The Religion of Israel
66. The Prophets
67. How Do We Know Jesus?
68. The Life of Our Lord
69. What is the Good News?
70. St. Paul and His Message
71. What the Old Testament Does Not Tell Us
72. The New Testament Apocrypha
73. Judaism

TWENTIETH CENTURY ENCYCLOPEDIA OF CATHOLICISM

PART SEVEN: THE HISTORY OF THE CHURCH

74. Christian Beginnings
75. The Dawn of the Middle Ages
76. The Early Middle Ages
77. The Later Middle Ages
78. Reformation and Counter-Reformation
79. The Church in the Modern Age

PART EIGHT: THE ORGANIZATION OF THE CHURCH

80. What is Canon Law?
81. The Papacy
82. The Ecumenical Councils
83. Successors of the Apostles
84. The Christian Priesthood
85. Religious Orders of Men
86. Religious Orders of Women
87. The Laity's Place in the Church
88. The Catholic Spirit

PART NINE: THE CHURCH AND THE MODERN WORLD

89. Church and State
90. Christianity and Economics
91. Contemporary Atheism
92. Science and Religion
93. Christianity and Psychiatry
94. Christianity and the Machine Age
95. Christianity and the Space Age
96. Christianity and Communism
97. Christianity and Colonialism
98. The Church Works Through Her Saints
99. History of the Missions
100. Missions in Modern Times
101. Religious Sociology
102. The Mission of the Church in the World
103. The Church and Sex
104. The Workers of the Church
105. Charity in Action
106. Christianity and Education
107. Why We Believe

PART TEN: THE WORSHIP OF THE CHURCH

108. The Spirit of Worship
109. The Books of Worship
110. History of the Mass
111. The Mass in the West
112. Eastern Liturgies
113. The Christian Calendar
114. Vestments and Church Furniture

PART ELEVEN: CATHOLICISM AND LITERATURE

115. What is a Christian Writer?
116. Sacred Languages
117. Christian Humanism
118. Christianity and Modern Thought
119. Modern Christian Literature

PART TWELVE: CATHOLICISM AND THE ARTS

120. The Christian Meaning of Art
121. The Origins of Christian Art
122. Church Building
123. Christian Painting and Sculpture
124. Christian Theatre
125. Christian Music
126. Motion Pictures, Radio and Television

PART THIRTEEN: CATHOLICISM AND SCIENCE

127. Embryo and Anima
128. Nuclear Physics in Peace and War
129. Medicine and Morals
130. To be assigned
131. To be assigned
132. To be assigned
133. To be assigned

PART FOURTEEN: OUTSIDE THE CHURCH

134. Judaism and the Law
135. Greek and Russian Orthodoxy
136. Heresies and Heretics
137. Protestantism
138. The Ecumenical Movement
139. Modern Sects

PART FIFTEEN: NON-CHRISTIAN BELIEFS

140. Primitive Religions
141. Religions of the Ancient East
142. Greco-Roman Religion
143. The Religion of Mohammed
144. Hinduism
145. Buddhism
146. Mystery Cults
147. Superstition
148. The Rationalists

PART SIXTEEN: GENERAL AND SUPPLEMENTARY VOLUMES

149. Why I am a Christian
150. Index

All titles are subject to change.